e About

USINESS

More About
This Business
of Music

More About This Business of Music

SIDNEY SHEMEL AND

M. WILLIAM KRASILOVSKY

edited by Lee Zhito

BILLBOARD
PUBLISHING COMPANY

To our children,
with affection

PREFACE

THIS book consists of additional topics and material not contained in *This Business of Music,* written by the same authors. The present volume has also been written in an attempt to help participants in the music and recording industries to comprehend the intricacies of the business and their rights and obligations. Economic facts deemed significant for daily operations as well as common legal concepts which guide business decisions are presented. The book is not designed to be a substitute for expert legal and accounting advice.

The authors wish to express their appreciation for the generous and valuable assistance received from many business associates and industry leaders. Special indebtedness is acknowledged to the following: Albert Berman, Morton M. Drosnes, Walter A. Evans, Hy Faine, Sylvia Goldstein, Frank Hackinson, David Hall, William M. Kaplan, Leon Kellman, Don O'Neill, Carl Sigmon, Benjamin Starr, Alan J. Stein and the firm of Orenstein, Arrow & Lourie. The staff of *Billboard*, including Hal B. Cook, Lee Zhito, Andrew J. Csida and Sidney Horowitz, has been most helpful. Special appreciation is due to Lee Zhito for his editing and for his material contribution to the chapter on Tape Cartridges.

The gratitude expressed in this acknowledgment does not imply the responsibility of anyone but the authors for the contents of this book.

CONTENTS

PART TWO **Other Aspects of the Music Industry**

PART THREE **Appendix**

More About
This Business
of Music

PART ONE

THE BUSINESS
OF SERIOUS MUSIC

1

BACKGROUND

THE field of serious music is commonly considered to include symphonies, chamber music, operas, choral works, oratorios, piano sonatas and other recital pieces. There are the established repertoire works of Bach, Beethoven and Brahms and the more contemporary compositions of Barber, Copland, Bartók, Bloch, Shostakovich, Stravinsky and Schoenberg. Included are the famous Italian operas written by Rossini, Puccini and Verdi and the recent operas by Gian-Carlo Menotti.

SYMPHONY ORCHESTRAS

America is considered to be a country of quality symphony orchestras. The 1,401 symphony orchestras in the United States in 1965 made up more than half of the world's total symphony orchestras. The United States has five orchestras (New York, Philadelphia, Boston, Cleveland and Chicago) which are reputed to be of as high calibre as Europe's leading orchestras (the Vienna and Berlin Philharmonics and the Amsterdam Concertgebouw). Even the orchestras from the smaller American cities are regarded favorably in comparison with their European counterparts.

The plight of serious musicians is reflected by the fact that in 1964 the average contract salary for the musicians of major orchestras was a little more than $5,000. With the exception of the country's few major and metropolitan orchestras, the orchestra musicians earn an average of a few hundred dollars per year. Most symphony orchestras have seasons which are less than 30 weeks. Year-round contracts are offered by only the Philadelphia, Boston, New York, Chicago and Cleveland orchestras.

Musicians generally must find outside employment in music or other fields to supplement their income as serious musicians. Of the 60,000 persons who in 1964 played regularly in the 1,401 symphony orchestras in the United States, only about 7,200 persons were professionals. With respect to the 1,401 orchestras, 288 were college and university orchestras, 1,059 were community orchestras operating on annual budgets under $100,000, 29 were metropolitan orchestras with budgets from $100,000 to $500,000, and 25 were so-called major orchestras with budgets over $500,000. Only the 54 metropolitan and major orchestras were composed predominantly of professional musicians.

OPERA GROUPS

In 1964, there were 754 opera-producing groups, of which 35 to 40 were fully professional. Not more than 10 of the groups provided performances more than 15 days a year. Of the 754 organizations, 227 were within the music departments of universities. Other than the New York Metropolitan Opera, the New York City Opera, the Chicago Lyric Opera, the San Francisco Opera and two or three special operatic groups, there is little or no professional opera in the United States during most of the year.

Operatic records represented 25 per cent of all 1965 dollar sales of serious music recordings in the United States.

DEFICITS OF ORCHESTRAS AND OPERA GROUPS

Most performing arts organizations, including symphony orchestras and opera groups, operate at a deficit and depend on contributions to survive. The nation's 25 major symphony orchestras in the 1963-1964 season derived about 52 per cent of their total expenses from ticket sales. Of the $49 million spent by United States symphony orchestras in the 1963-1964 year, about $20 million, or 41 per cent was raised from sources other than earned income; roughly $12 million was contributed by individuals and business firms. For the few major opera companies, the box office provided an average of 70 per cent of operating costs.

Broadcasting and recording add significantly to the total income of the Metropolitan Opera and the Boston, New York and Philadelphia symphony orchestras. Of its aggregate income in the 1963-1964 year, the

Boston orchestra received about 8 per cent from record sales, and the Philadelphia orchestra approximately 12.5 per cent. This is unusual. Only six of the 25 major symphony orchestras add substantially to their box office earnings by broadcasting or recordings.

It has been estimated by Samuel R. Rosenbaum, trustee of the Recording Industries Music Performance Trust Funds, that persons who buy tickets for the live professional performing arts do not exceed one per cent of the population.

GOVERNMENT'S INTEREST

Composer Aaron Copland has stated that "Music as everybody knows has always been the last of the arts to flower in any country. In its primitive or folk form, there is nothing more natural to man, but in its cultivated form it seems to need more coddling than any of its sister arts."

Many countries in the Western world, including Great Britain, France, Germany, Italy, Sweden and Canada, directly subsidize serious music. This has not been true of the United States government until very recently.

The United States government's increasing concern for the performing arts is indicated by the enactment on September 29, 1965, of a Federal statute establishing a National Foundation on the Arts and the Humanities. Its purpose is developing and promoting a national policy for the arts and humanities.

The statute marks a significant departure from the prior policy of depending almost entirely on private philanthropy and State activities. Some indirect assistance from the Federal government was extended through income tax benefits to private individuals and firms for their contributions in support of the arts.

GOVERNMENT ENDOWMENTS

Under the statute, the Foundation has two major branches, called Endowments: a National Endowment for the Arts, and a National Endowment for the Humanities. Each Endowment is given guidance and advice by Councils of Private Citizens, appointed by the President. For the Arts Endowment, the advisory body is the National Council on the Arts, established by statute during 1964, and composed of 26 private citizens plus its Chairman. The Council Chairman serves as the chief executive officer of the Endowment. Coordination between the two Endowments is provided through a Federal Council on the Arts and the Humanities.

The general guidelines for the activities to be supported by the National Endowment for the Arts are broad in scope and include the following:

(1) Productions which have substantial artistic and cultural significance, giving emphasis to American creativity and the maintenance and encouragement of professional excellence;

(2) Productions, meeting professional standards or standards of authenticity, irrespective of origin, which are of significant merit and which, without such assistance, would otherwise be unavailable to our citizens in many areas of the country;

(3) Projects that will encourage and assist artists and enable them to achieve standards of professional excellence;

(4) Workshops that will encourage and develop the appreciation and enjoyment of the arts by our citizens; and

(5) Other relevant projects, including surveys, research, and planning in the arts.

For the purpose of the Arts Endowment, the definition of "arts" is comprehensive and includes the following:

"Music (instrumental and vocal), dance, drama, folk art, creative writing, architecture and allied fields, painting, sculpture, photography, graphic and craft arts, industrial design, costume and fashion design, motion pictures, television, radio, tape and sound recording, and the arts related to the presentation, performance, execution, and exhibition of such major art forms."

The Arts Endowment was originally authorized $5,000,000 by Congress for each of the fiscal years 1956, 1967 and 1968, and thereafter authorizations would be subject to review by Congress. In order to stimulate private philanthropy for cultural endeavors and State activities to benefit the arts, an additional $2,250,000 for the Arts Endowment was originally authorized to match funds donated by private sources. Also, $2,750,000 was authorized for the Arts Endowment to enable each of the States (55 entities in all, including the District of Columbia and outlying areas) having a State arts agency to receive an annual grant of up to $50,000 on an even-matching basis. In most cases, grants are limited to 50 per cent of the total cost of a project. Although the appropriations have been substantial, pursuant to Congressional budgetary controls, there have been some subsequent reductions in the funds made available for the activities of the Arts Endowment.

EMPLOYMENT OUTLOOK

The prospects for employment of musicians and singers are indicated in a 1963-1964 report by the Department of Labor on Employment Outlook in the Performing Arts. The sections relating to Musicians and Music Teachers and to Singers and Singing Teachers are included as Appendix A. The report states in part:

> "As a field of employment, instrumental music has been overcrowded for many years, and it is expected to remain so throughout the 1960's.

> "Employment opportunities for performers are not expected to increase over the long run."

As to singers, the report states:

> "The employment situation for singers will probably remain highly competitive during the remainder of the 1960's.

> "Little growth in overall employment opportunities for performers is likely over the long run."

UNION SCALE

The difficult, intermittent and seasonal employment situation of symphony orchestra musicians, the supply of which is generally larger than the demand for their services, has been recognized by the American Federation of Musicians in its agreement with phonograph record companies.

The following table compares the American Federation of Musicians standards for symphonic and popular music:

	SYMPHONIC	POPULAR
Minimum session	2 hours	3 hours
Permissible recording at session	40 minutes	15 minutes
Pay scale per session in 1966	$50.38	$61.00
Overtime pay per one-half hour	$12.60	$20.33

There is a minimum call basic session of two hours for symphonic recordings, as compared to three hours for other recordings. Furthermore, the record company can complete forty minutes of recorded symphonic music, in contrast to only fifteen minutes of popular album music. The musician's pay scale of $50.38 in 1966 for a symphonic session is roughly

17 per cent lower than the $61.00 payable for a popular music session. The half-hour overtime rate of $12.60 for symphony orchestra musicians is 38 per cent lower than the $20.33 for popular music musicians.

In reality, the 17 per cent difference in basic session pay is on the low side, in terms of productivity as measured by the greater amount of finished music that can result from the two-hour symphonic music session.

The American Federation of Television and Radio Artists, which represents singers who make phonograph recordings, also makes concessions with respect to serious music. In its agreement with phonograph record companies, the union predicates hourly pay on an average of up to 5 minutes of finished recorded music for each hour of a serious music session, whereas for popular music an hour's pay is due for each 3½ minutes of finished music. For finished recorded music in excess of these limits, a singer receives one-fourth hour's pay for each additional 1¼ minutes of classical music or part thereof; for popular music, an additional 50 per cent of the 3½ minute rate is paid for each 60 seconds or portion thereof over 3½ minutes.

A distinction is also made as to pay scale for coach rehearsal of singing groups of 25 or more. For serious music recordings, a coach rehearsal not in excess of 1½ hours and contiguous to the recording session may be called, and the scale pay is $6 per hour per singer, which is 50 per cent of the regular recording pay. For popular music, rehearsal pay is the same as regular recording pay.

RECORDING INDUSTRY TRUST FUNDS

For many years, the producers of phonograph records, electrical transcriptions and television film have been contributing to the Recording Industries Music Performance Trust Funds pursuant to agreements negotiated with the American Federation of Musicians. Most of the contributions have been made by the phonograph record industry on the basis of percentages of the suggested retail list price of records sold.

Payments to the Funds in recent years have been in excess of $5,000,000 a year. Collections are expended currently. The expenditures have been made for free concerts in the United States and Canada to encourage work by musicians at union scale, and to foster the educational and cultural life of the nations. In the first half of 1965, almost $700,000 was spent for concerts of chamber and symphonic music; the Trust Funds have thereby aided several hundred civic symphony orchestras in the United States and Canada.

Pursuant to the 1964-1969 agreement between the American Federation of Musicians and the recording industry, half of the contributions of the phonograph record industry go into a Special Fund for distribution to the musicians who participated in creating the new recordings. The balance is used for free concerts.

2

ORGANIZATIONS AND REPRESENTATIVES

THE FIELD of serious music includes a number of important unions and other organizations, some of which have been previously mentioned.

The American Federation of Musicians ("AFM") takes jurisdiction over musicians in symphony, opera and ballet orchestras.

Solo operatic singers, solo concert artists (both instrumentalists and singers) and choral singers in the operatic and concert fields are members of the American Guild of Musical Artists ("AGMA").

Singers engaged in light opera (and musical comedy) are members of Actors' Equity Association.

Vocal performers who sing for phonograph records are under the aegis of the American Federation of Television and Radio Artists ("AFTRA"), irrespective of their membership in other unions. Similarly, instrumentalists who record for phonograph records, whether or not they are members of other unions, belong to the American Federation of Musicians.

All of the above unions except the AFM are branches of the Associated Actors and Artistes of America (AFL-CIO).

An organization of serious music composers is the American Composers Alliance, which has made special agreements with Broadcast Music, Inc., a performing right organization described hereinafter, with respect to the performance of the Alliance's members' music. Another organization of serious music composers is the American Music Center, Inc., which acts as an information center and as a loan library for its members' works. Both organizations are described more fully hereinafter.

The American Guild of Authors and Composers ("AGAC") is open to both popular and serious music writers. It has a present membership of over 2,000 writers and has entered into agreements with more than 1,000 publishers. This minority of publishers is bound to use the standard contract of AGAC in dealing with AGAC members. Because of the special problems of serious music writers, the Guild and the American Composers Alliance have been studying the advisability of a different form of contract for serious music writers. The Guild provides a service for its members through which it watches over copyrights, and at the appropriate time it files applications with the Copyright Office for their renewals. All AGAC members permit the Guild, for a service fee of 4½ per cent, to collect and audit the royalties payable to AGAC members by publishers.

The organization of the standard music publishers is the Music Publishers' Association of the United States, to which most of the important publishers belong. A list of the members of the Association is included as Appendix B.

PERFORMING RIGHT SOCIETIES

There are three performing right organizations in America, the American Society of Composers, Authors and Publishers ("ASCAP"), Broadcast Music, Inc. ("BMI") and SESAC, Inc. ASCAP is a membership organization of some 8,200 composers and authors and 2,700 publishers. It was founded in 1914, and shares revenue equally between writers and publishers.

BMI, a competitor of ASCAP, represents about 10,300 writers and over 7,100 publishers. BMI is owned by some 300 broadcasting stations. It was established by the broadcasters in 1940 in order to increase broadcasting industry bargaining power with ASCAP. Except for operating expenses and reserves, all of BMI's collections are paid to its affiliated publishers and writers, with no dividends to the owners of BMI.

SESAC is a private performing right licensing organization which has been owned by the Heinecke family for over 30 years. SESAC represents some 100 active publishers who control about 300 catalogs. Payments by SESAC are made solely to publisher affiliates and not to writers. It is generally accepted that SESAC's position is relatively minor in comparison with that of ASCAP or BMI.

OTHER ORGANIZATIONS

The American Symphony Orchestra League, founded in 1942, is a non-profit, membership, service and research organization in which voting memberships are held by major, metropolitan, community and college symphony orchestras and arts councils. About two-thirds of the symphony orchestras in the United States are represented within the membership. Non-voting individual memberships are held by symphony orchestra conductors, musicians, managers, members of symphony orchestra boards and symphony women's associations, educational organizations, music business firms and libraries.

The National Music Council, founded as a non-profit membership corporation in 1940 and chartered by the United States Congress in 1957, is comprised of some 55 member musical associations of national scope. These represent an aggregate individual membership of more than 1,250,000.

It was organized, and provides a forum, for the discussion of the United States' national musical affairs and problems. It constitutes a clearinghouse for the opinions and decisions of, and information concerning, its member organizations. It coordinates the efforts of its member organizations. It acts to enhance the importance of music in the national life and culture. In the *National Music Council Bulletin,* issued three times a year, there is news about its member organizations, accounts of governmental activities in the field of music, digests of proposed congressional legislation regarding music, lists of musical competitions and contests, and articles on music in industry.

The Council is the sole musical society among the national groups represented on the United States Commission for UNESCO. A list of the organizations which belong to the National Music Council is included as Appendix C.

MANAGERS AND AGENTS

Performing artists in the field of serious music usually obtain employment through managers who are sometimes referred to as booking agents. Included in this field are large firms such as Columbia Artists Management, Inc., Hurok Attractions, Inc., and the William Morris Agency, Inc., as well as a considerable number of individual managers with more limited facilities.

As previously noted, artists in the fields of opera, concert, recital and oratorio (as well as dance and ballet) are represented by the American Guild of Musical Artists ("AGMA"). By an agreement between managers and artists, the union regulates managers' relationships with its members.

A list of some 45 persons and firms who as managers have entered into an agreement with AGMA is set forth as Appendix D. The term for any management contract, including renewal and option obligations, cannot exceed four years, and there are minimum terms under which an artist can be made available for engagements. The artist has the right to terminate the agreement with a manager in the absence of certain minimum earnings during the first year of management or if specified personnel leave the manager's employ.

The standard form of artist management contract required by AGMA for its members is included as Appendix E. This form provides that maximum fees of managers range from 10 per cent of gross receipts for operatic, radio and phonograph record engagements to 20 per cent of gross receipts for regular concert engagements. A maximum fee of 15 per cent of gross receipts is applicable to civic, community and similarly organized concert engagements.

AGMA does not regulate its approximately 5,000 members in their dealings with personal representatives who are not also managers. Such persons, who will handle accounting, investments and other career guidance matters, do not necessarily duplicate the role of managers whose functions center upon the negotiation of employment agreements and related activities, such as collection of payments.

When an AGMA member deals with a major institutional employer, such as the Metropolitan Opera Company, the basic terms are laid out by the union and the employer in a collectively bargained agreement covering all union members. In 1965, opera companies under AGMA agreements numbered nearly 70. Similar agreements are made with professional choruses and symphony associations.

The AGMA standard artist's form of contract for employment is included as Appendix F. This standard agreement is subject to modifications contained in basic agreements between AGMA and a particular employer.

Occasionally a concert artist, although an AGMA member, will find it necessary to join other unions. For example, vocal recording artists are governed by the American Federation of Television and Radio Artists. When duplicate union membership is required among the performing unions which are branches of the Associated Actors and Artistes of America (AFL-CIO), arrangements are made for the first union joined ("parent" union) to receive its full initiation fee and dues, and for the second union to accept less than its usual fees and dues.

3

RECORDING INDUSTRY ASPECTS

Lovers of serious music are wooed by various record companies, some of which are well known for the quality of their classical recordings. Many serious music recordings, both excellent and of lesser quality, originate in Europe. This is due to the traditional European interest in such music, and also because Europe's lower wage scales make it more economically feasible to record large symphony orchestras, choral and operatic groups there. European recording may cost as little as one-third of the amount it would cost to record the same compositions with an orchestra of like size in America.

SALE OF RECORDINGS

Serious music accounted for 9.9 per cent of America's $598,000,000 long-playing record sales in 1965. The following two charts are based on 1965 United States record sales figures. Chart I shows the share of serious music in total United States record sales. Chart II presents the share of serious music record sales in the United States of different LP price categories.

Various American and European record labels shared in these sales. Lists of serious music labels and LP's are contained in the Schwann Long Playing Record Catalogs. Famous serious music record trademarks from Europe include Deutsche Grammophon, Telefunken and Electrola from Germany, Pathé Marconi from France, Cetra from Italy, and Angel and

Chart I

THE SHARE OF SERIOUS MUSIC
IN TOTAL U.S.A. RECORD SALES
(Based on 1965 Figures)

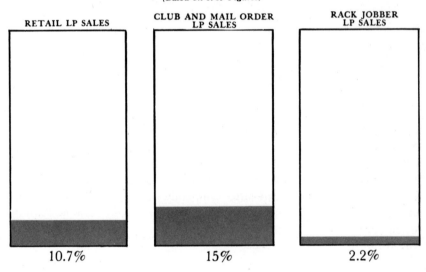

RETAIL LP SALES   CLUB AND MAIL ORDER LP SALES   RACK JOBBER LP SALES

10.7%   15%   2.2%

Chart II

SHARE OF SERIOUS MUSIC RECORD SALES
IN U.S.A. BY PRICE CATEGORIES
(Based on 1965 Figures)

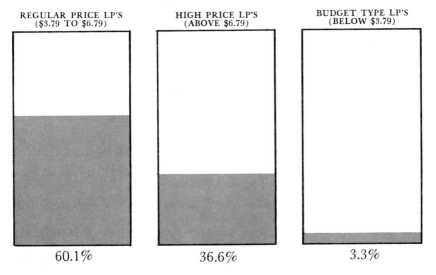

REGULAR PRICE LP'S ($3.79 TO $6.79)	HIGH PRICE LP'S (ABOVE $6.79)	BUDGET TYPE LP'S (BELOW $3.79)
60.1%	36.6%	3.3%

London from England. Respected serious music records also appear on RCA Victor, Capitol and Columbia, which are among the largest American record companies. There are other reputable American companies which also issue serious music recordings.

European labels are customarily handled by the larger American record companies and are usually not directly released in the United States by the European companies. This is explained in large part by the fact that the more substantial European companies are in many instances affiliated through common ownership with the American companies.

For example, the Telefunken and London labels are in the British Decca group, which also includes London Records. The Electrola label is a part of the E.M.I. combine which includes Capitol Records, as are also the Angel and Pathé Marconi labels. Philips classical records are issued by Mercury Record Corp. which is affiliated with N. V. Philips Phonographische Industrie of Holland. Deutsche Grammophon recordings continue to be released through MGM Records, despite the fact that Deutsche Grammophon is linked with Philips of Holland and Mercury Record Corp. of the United States.

PRICE CATEGORIES

Higher priced serious music recordings usually have suggested list prices of $4.79 for monaural LP's, and $5.79 for stereophonic LP's. Budget line suggested list prices vary from about $.98 to $2.98, with the $1.98 and $2.50 product accounting for the lion's share of the lower cost market. The major growth appears to be in the $1.98 field.

RCA Victor affixes its Red Seal label to the higher priced recordings, and uses its Camden and Victrola labels for the budget recordings. London Records' London label is comparable to the RCA Red Seal label. London's lower priced records bear the Richmond trademark.

Capitol issues higher priced recordings on its Capitol Classics and Angel labels, and its budget recordings on the Promenade label. The Decca trademark appears on its better classical recordings, and the Vocalion mark on its budget line. Mercury has the Mercury label for more expensive recordings, and employs the Wing and Country labels for budget records.

Budget lines, which are released by both large and small companies, do not necessarily signify lower quality. Frequently they are top-grade recordings of older vintage with established artists and conductors.

For example, there was hailed recently the first Beethoven Ninth

Symphony recording to appear in stereo on a low-priced label, RCA Victor's Victrola. The conductor on this seven-year-old recording is Charles Munch and the orchestra the Boston Symphony. It also features an outstanding quartet of vocalists, including Leontyne Price. The record was withdrawn from the full price catalog only two years before its issuance in the budget line.

Some budget lines, such as Nonesuch, Music Guild and Turnabout, specialize in esoteric recordings, with emphasis on baroque music.

It is possible to find the identical artists and conductors being featured in both price categories at the same time. In fact, the discriminating record buyer who is not seeking the most recent recordings may find that he can build an excellent record library founded on low priced recordings.

Price discounting is as rampant in serious music recordings as it is in other types of recordings. *The New York Times* Sunday edition frequently runs advertisements of cut-price sales. E. J. Korvette, Sam Goody, Inc. and The Record Hunter are stores which advertise from time to time.

The wealth of budget labels available and the extent of discounting may be illustrated by the advertisement on the next page, from a Sunday issue of *The New York Times*. On the same day, E. J. Korvette announced that it was selling $4.79 suggested list-priced records for $2.34, $5.79 list-priced recordings for $2.84, and $6.79 records for $3.34.

RECORD CLUBS

All of the substantial mail order record clubs in the United States deal in classical records. Among the leading record clubs are the Columbia Record Club, RCA Victor Record Club, Capitol Record Club, Record Club of America, Reader's Digest, Longines Symphonette, and Citadel. The largest club is the Columbia Record Club, which has close to 2,000,000 members.

In the case of the Columbia, RCA and Capitol Clubs, the subscriber usually receives a certain number of records at below-cost prices upon agreeing to buy a given number of additional selections at regular club prices during the next 12 months. After the initial year, the member, depending on the particular club, is induced to continue his membership by being accorded either the right to buy records at discounted prices, or the right to receive free or bonus records for each given number of records that he purchases.

The three clubs handle the records of several record labels, including those of their namesake record company. These clubs ordinarily take

master tapes from their licensing record companies and then press records based on the tapes. They pay royalties to the licensing record company, mechanical copyright license fees to the copyright proprietor, and make payments on sales due to the Music Performance Trust Fund and the Special Fund. The licensing record company pays any artist royalties which become due.

Certain clubs, such as the Record Club of America and the Citadel Record Club, sell all records listed in the comprehensive Schwann LP record catalog at a discount of about one-third off the suggested retail list price. There is no obligation to buy a minimum number of records. These clubs sell finished product which they buy. They thereby incur no pressing, copyright, artist or American Federation of Musicians union obligations in their operations.

Recordings of new classical albums by leading record companies have been encouraged by the additional sales anticipated through their record club affiliations.

TRADE REVIEWS

New serious music recordings are reviewed extensively in *Billboard* and to a lesser extent in *Cash Box,* record and music publishing weekly trade papers. *Variety* and *Record World,* which review popular music recordings weekly, do not usually contain serious music reviews.

Billboard in its Album Reviews places recordings in one of the following categories: CLASSICAL SPOTLIGHT, LOW PRICE CLASSICAL SPOTLIGHT, CLASSICAL SPECIAL MERIT, FOUR-STAR or THREE-STAR. The CLASSICAL SPOTLIGHT and CLASSICAL LOW PRICE SPOTLIGHT ratings indicate recordings of outstanding merit with sufficient sales potential to become a top seller in their categories. Recordings rated CLASSICAL SPECIAL MERIT are regarded as deserving of exposure and ones which could have commercial success. Albums which are rated FOUR-STAR or THREE-STAR are considered to have lower sales potential. *Cash Box* in its Album Reviews has a rating called CLASSICAL PICKS. In each issue of *Cash Box* two classical albums are given that rating. No other review of classical albums appears. *Billboard* prints weekly charts listing BEST SELLING CLASSICAL LP's in retail outlets. A typical weekly chart issued by *Billboard* is reproduced below:

BEST SELLING CLASSICAL LP's

This Week	Last Week	Title, Artist, Label & No.	Weeks on Chart
Billboard Award	5	**BERNSTEIN CONDUCTS IVES** N. Y. Phil. (Bernstein), Col. ML 6243 (M); MS 6843 (S)	5
2	1	**VERDI: DON CARLO (4-12" LP)** Tebaldi, Bumbry, Lon. A 4432 (M); OSA 1432 (S)	12
3	2	**PRESENTING MONTSERRAT CABALLE** RCA LM 2862 (M); LSC 2862 (S)	12
4	3	**MAHLER: SYMPHONY NO. 4 IN G** Cleve. Orch. (Szell), Col. PL 6233 (M); MS 6833 (S)	12
5	8	**BRAHMS: LIEBESLIEDER WALTZES** Shaw Chorale, RCA LM 2864 (M); LSC 2864 (S)	11
6	6	**MAHLER: SYMPHONY NO. 10 (2-12" LP)** Phila. Orch. (Ormandy), Col. M2L 335 (M); M2S 735 (S)	12
7	4	**IVES: SYMPHONY NO. 4** Amer. Symph. Orch. (Stokowski), Col. ML 6175 (M); MS 6775 (S)	12
8	7	**CHOPIN WALTZES** Rubinstein, RCA LM 2726 (M); LSC 2726 (S)	12
9	14	**IVES: SYMPHONY NO. 1** Chicago Symph. Orch. (Gould), RCA LM 2893 (M); LSC 2893 (S)	4
10	13	**NIELSEN: SYMPHONY NO. 3** Royal Danish Orch. (Bernstein), Col. ML 6169 (M); MS 6769 (S)	12
11	10	**BLESS THIS HOUSE** Mormon Tab. Choir/Phila. Orch. (Ormandy), Col. ML 6235 (M); MS 6835 (S)	12
12	20	**ZARZUELA ARIAS** Caballe, RCA LM 2894 (M); LSC 2894 (S)	3
13	15	**BRAHMS: DEUTSCHE VOLKSLIEDER (2-12" LP)** Schwarzkopf, Fischer-Dieskau & Moore, Angel B 3675 (M); SB 3675 (S)	7
14	16	**SOUVENIR OF A GOLDEN ERA (2-12" LP)** Horne, Lon. A 4263 (M); OSA 1263 (S)	5
15	9	**RODRIGO: CONCIERTO DE ARANJUEZ/TEDESCO: CONCERTO IN D** Williams, Col. ML 6234 (M); MS 6834 (S)	12
16	21	**BAROQUE GUITAR** Bream, RCA LM 2878 (M); LSC 2878 (S)	9
17	17	**HOLIDAY FOR STRINGS** Boston Pops (Fiedler), RCA LM 2885 (M); LSC 2885 (S)	12
18	12	**BACH ON THE PEDAL HARPSICHORD** Biggs, Col. ML 6204 (M); MS 6804 (S)	9
19	19	**REVERIE** Phila. Orch. (Ormandy), Col. ML 5975 (M); MS 6575 (S)	11
20	11	**MY FAVORITE CHOPIN** Cliburn, RCA LM 2576 (M); LSC 2576 (S)	12
21	18	**HOROWITZ AT CARNEGIE HALL—AN HISTORIC RETURN (2-12" LP)** Col. M2L 328 (M); M2S 728 (S)	12
22	28	**MUSSORGSKY-STOKOWSKI: PICTURES AT AN EXHIBITION** New Philm. Orch. (Stokowski), Lon. PM 55004 (M); SPC 21006 (S)	12
23	23	**LISZT: SONATA IN B MINOR/SCHUBERT: WANDERER FANTASY** Rubinstein, RCA LM 2871 (M); LSC 2871 (S)	7
24	25	**THE BAROQUE OBOE** Gomberg/Col. Chamber Orch. (Ozawa), Col. ML 6232 (M); MS 6832 (S)	12
25	22	**BIZET: CARMEN (3-12" LP)** Callas, Gedda & Various Artists, Angel CLX 3650 (M); SCLX 3650 (S)	8
26	30	**GERSHWIN: RHAPSODY IN BLUE** N. Y. Phil. (Bernstein), Col. ML 5413 (M); MS 6091 (S)	12
27	29	**BRUCKNER: SYMPHONY NO. 9 IN D MINOR** Vienna Philm. (Mehta), Lon. CM 9462 (M); CS 6462 (S)	6
28	27	**TCHAIKOVSKY: CONCERTO NO. 1** Cliburn, RCA LM 2252 (M); LSC 2252 (S)	12
29	32	**ROSSINI: WILLIAM TELL OVERTURE** N. Y. Phil. (Bernstein), Col. ML 6143 (M); MS 6743 (S)	10
30	31	**MOZART: SYMPHONIES NOS. 29 & 33** New Philm. Orch. (Klemperer), Angel 36329 (M); S 36329 (S)	2
31	33	**GERSHWIN: RHAPSODY IN BLUE/AMERICAN IN PARIS** Lon. Fest. Orch. (Black), Lon. (No Mono); SPC 21009 (S)	7
32	24	**PUCCINI: LA BOHEME (2-12" LP)** Freni, Gedda & Various Artists, Angel BL 3643 (M); SBL 3643 (S)	7
33	—	**PURCELL: MUSIC FOR THE THEATER** Bath Fest. Orch. (Menuhin), Angel 36332 (M); S 36332 (S)	1
34	—	**MAHLER: SYMPHONY NO. 6 (2-12" LP)** Boston Symph. (Leinsdorf), RCA LM 7044 (M); LSC 7044 (S)	1
35	40	**RITUAL FIRE DANCE** Phila. Orch. (Ormandy), Col. ML 6223 (M); MS 6823 (S)	2
36	39	**MOZART: SYMPHONIES NOS. 28 & 33** Cleve. Orch. (Szell), Col. ML 6258 (M); MS 6858 (S)	3
37	—	**E. POWER BIGGS PLAYS MOZART—MUSIC FOR SOLO ORGAN** Col. ML 6256 (M); MS 6856 (S)	1
38	—	**BEETHOVEN: CONCERTO NO. 5 ("Emperor")** G. Gould/Amer. Symph. Orch. (Stokowski), Col. ML 6288 (M); MS 6888 (S)	1
39	—	**BARTOK: CONCERTO FOR ORCHESTRA** Cleve. Orch. (Szell), Col. ML 6215 (M); MS 6815 (S)	5
40	37	**SONGS OF THE AUVERGNE** Moffo, Amer. Symph. Orch. (Stokowski), RCA LM 2795 (M); LSC 2795 (S)	3

NEW ACTION LP's

RACHMANINOFF: PIANO CONCERTO NO. 2/TCHAIKOVSKY: PIANO CONCERTO NO. 1 . . . .
 Janis, Minn. Symph. Orch. (Dorati)/Lon. Symph. Orch. (Menges), Merc. MG 50448 (M); SR 90448 (S)

BEST SELLING BUDGET-LINE LP's

This Week

1. **STRAVINSKY: SACRE DU PRINTEMPS (Rite of Spring)**—R.T.F. Orch. Intl. (Boulez), Nonesuch H 1093 (M); H 71093 (S)
2. **NIELSEN: CONCERTO FOR VIOLIN**—Varga, Royal Danish Orch. (Semkow), Turnabout TV 4043 (M); TV 34043 (S)
3. **LISZT: MAZEPPA**—Hungarian St. Con. Orch. (Nemeth), Mace 9009 (M); S 9009 (S)
4. **BRAHMS: GERMAN REQUIEM (2-12" LP)**—Stich-Randall, Pease & Various Artists, Nonesuch H 3003 (M); H 73003 (S)
5. **BERWALD: 2 QUINTETS FOR PIANO**—Riefling, Benthien Qr., Nonesuch H 1113 (M); H 71113 (S)
6. **BEETHOVEN: FIDELIO (2-12" LP)**—Kuchta, Patzak & Various Artists, (Nonesuch H 3005 (M); H 73005 (S)
7. **MUSSORGSKY: PICTURES AT AN EXHIBITION**—Vienna St. Op. Orch. (Golschmann), Everyman SRV 117 (M); SRV 117 SD (S)
8. **MASCAGNI: CAVALLERIA RUSTICANA (2-12" LP)**—Del Monaco, Ghione, Richmond R 62008 (M); (No Stereo)
9. **RIMSKY-KORSAKOV: SCHEHERAZADE**—Lon. Symph. Orch. (Monteux), RCA Victrola VIC 1013 (M); VICS 1013 (S)
10. **ELECTRONIC MUSIC**—Various Artists, Turnabout TV 4046 (M); TV 34046 (S)

CONSUMER PUBLICATION REVIEWS

Reviews of classical albums are carried in various magazines, including *High Fidelity, Hi Fi Stereo Review, Harpers, American Record Guide* and *Saturday Review*, and in the Sunday edition of *The New York Times* and other key daily newspapers.

RECORDING ARTISTS

The factor of prestige may loom large in negotiations by record companies for the services of renowned serious music artists and orchestras. Their recordings draw public attention to the company, and may also attract interest in other albums in its catalog.

Another element in negotiations is the long active life of many serious music recordings; this in contrast to the short life of most popular music LP's. On the other hand, serious music LP sales may be considerably slower than the sales of a popular music album, so that it may take much longer to recoup the recording company's investment.

Serious music has charms for the listening public in many countries of the world, whereas the sales of a popular album may be restricted to only a few countries. An Arturo Toscanini conducted symphony orchestra LP will sell for years and has a wide international market. In its calculations, the record company may also be influenced by the fact that no mechanical license royalties will be payable for public domain music contained in an album, and that copyrighted serious music can be customarily licensed at rates lower than those applicable to popular music.

A recording contract with a serious music artist is similar in many respects to the contract entered into with a popular music artist. The contract will provide that the artist's services are exclusive to the record company for all phonograph record recordings. The term of the agreement will be at least one year, and there are likely to be a number of one-year extension options in favor of the record company. These options are exercisable by a notice in writing to the artist before the expiration of the prior one-year term.

The popular artist and the serious music artist are treated differently in a number of respects. The serious music artist is usually only an album seller and there is little or no expectation that he will have sales of other types of records. The minimum number of recordings set forth in the agreement with a serious music artist will be in terms of the number of LP's rather than, as in the case of the popular artist, the number of single sides to be recorded.

Another difference may relate to the recoupability of the recording costs of the album from the artist's royalties. Such costs are usually recoupable from the artist's royalties in the case of a popular artist. If the serious music artist is a solo pianist performer, such as Arthur Rubinstein or Claudio Arrau, there are no recording costs of consequence other than studio costs. It is probably immaterial to the record company that it relinquish the right to recoup recording costs from the artist's royalties. A similar observation might apply to instrumentalists or vocalists who may use only a piano accompaniment.

On the other hand, the costs of recording the average album by a symphony orchestra comes to about $20,000. Whether recording costs of serious music recordings are recoupable from the artist royalties is the subject of negotiations in each instance. However, as compared to popular music recordings, it is more common to find that, except for the union scale paid to a featured artist, the record company has waived the right to recoup out of the artist royalties. This is more prevalent in the case of established performers and the better symphony orchestras which have devoted record audiences that assure the company of substantial sales.

While the upper limit of royalties payable to popular music artists tends to be 5 per cent of the suggested retail list price, less the price of packaging, royalties of 10 per cent to the serious music artist for recordings of public domain music are not unusual. A provision is often made that the royalty rate for recordings of copyrighted music will be lower. Royalties of 6 per cent for copyrighted music recordings are common.

Here again the more favorable terms will be given to the artist or orchestra which has an extensive record following. As a part of the negotiations, the company and the artist will also discuss whether payments will be based on 90 per cent (as is common for popular artists) or a higher percentage of sales and whether the royalty rate will be reduced for sales outside the United States.

PUBLISHERS AND COMPOSERS

Serious music performers base much of their repertoire on the standard works by composers such as Bach, Beethoven, Brahms and Mozart. Much of this repertoire is in the public domain, and no performance fees or mechanical license fees can be collected for their performance or mechanical reproduction, but there is a steady and continuing interest in this music by students and performers. This is the foundation of the business of printing and selling editions of serious music from the public domain. Those engaged in this business know that they have no monopoly, and that they may anticipate competition from other publishers.

MUSIC PUBLISHERS

There are a few established music publishers in the United States which specialize in serious music. These include G. Schirmer, Inc., Carl Fischer, Inc., Galaxy Music Corp., Boosey & Hawkes, Inc. and C. F. Peters Corp.

Other large publishers have substantial educational music departments. Among these are Music Publishers Holding Corp., Mills Music, Southern Music Publishing Co., Inc., and Belwin, Inc. Publishers of serious music tend to be involved in significant printing operations, because the music is complex and the printed edition is important as the basis of studies by students and use by orchestras and individual performers.

All rights under copyright are available to publishers and writers of most twentieth century serious music. In the United States, there is copyright protection for the original 28 year period of copyright, and there is a copyright renewal period of an additional 28 years. Outside the United States, the duration of copyright is normally the author's lifetime plus 50 years. The latter period is likely to be longer than the duration of copyright protection in the United States. It is not unusual for this to result in serious music being in the public domain in the United States while it is still under copyright in other countries.

The more important rights under copyright are those of mechanically reproducing, performing, and printing the music. These will be considered in greater detail hereinafter. A form of publishing contract is included as Appendix G.

MECHANICAL RIGHTS

A composer will grant to a publisher the right to license the reproduction of the music by mechanical means, including tapes and records. In music trade parlance, the publisher grants a mechanical license to a record company.

In addition, the mechanical right is the basis for collecting synchronization fees. These are payable by the producers of motion pictures and television films for a license from the publisher to include copyrighted compositions in the soundtracks.

Serious music, as is popular music, is subject to the so-called compulsory licensing provisions of Section 1(e) of the Copyright Act of the United States. Under the terms thereof, once the copyright owner has used or permitted the use of a copyrighted composition for mechanical reproduction, then any other person may reproduce the music on payment to the copyright proprietor of a royalty of 2 cents "on each such part manufactured."

A person who intends to rely upon the compulsory license provision must serve a notice of such intention, by registered mail, upon the copyright owner, and a copy of the notice must also be sent to the Copyright Office in Washington, D.C. This is pursuant to the provisions of Section 101(e) of the Act.

While it has been argued that the word "part" in Section 1(e) means the entire record disc and that, thus, only 2 cents for an entire symphony would be payable to the copyright owner under the compulsory licensing provisions, this interpretation is vigorously opposed by the copyright proprietors of serious music. They contend this would misinterpret the intent of Congress.

In practice, users request and copyright owners grant mechanical licenses for serious music at the rate of one-quarter cent for each minute of playing time on a record. Thus, for an entire 40 minute album of serious music which is protected by copyright, the record company would pay a mechanical license fee of 10 cents. For a comparable popular music album containing 12 songs, a mechanical license at the compulsory license rate of 2 cents per composition would result in an aggregate license fee of 24 cents, or 140 per cent higher than the 10 cent rate for the serious music LP. As observed previously, this difference in the cost of mechanical license fees is an important factor in warranting higher royalty rates to the serious music artist.

Ordinarily, record companies do not resort to the compulsory licensing provisions of the Copyright Act. Thereunder, the copyright owner can require the manufacturer to furnish under oath on the 20th day of each month a report on the number of recordings manufactured during the prior month, and to pay royalties on records manufactured in any month by the 20th of the next succeeding month.

Under the usual license negotiated with music publishers, manufacturers are allowed to account for and pay royalties quarterly, instead of monthly. They are also commonly permitted to pay royalties on the number of records sold, rather than on the number manufactured. There is the possibility, too, of negotiating a license at a rate of less than 2 cents per composition.

Many serious music publishers are represented by the Harry Fox Office in New York City as their agent-trustee to administer mechanical licenses on their behalf. The same office frequently acts for the publisher in negotiating and issuing synchronization and performance licenses for theatrical and television motion pictures.

The Harry Fox Office can prove to be most helpful to producers of films in their obtaining proper licenses. It can and will supply a wealth of information as to the owners and proper licensors of copyrighted music.

As indicated previously, serious music may be in the public domain in the United States but be under copyright elsewhere. The Harry Fox Office represents many European publishers, one of whom may control the music for which film licenses are sought. A film producer will ordinarily apply for both a synchronization license and a United States performance license. He may rely on performance licenses granted to theatres outside the United States by local performing right organizations. He may also depend on the blanket licenses issued by such organizations to television stations in the United States and throughout most of the world. In the United States, the theatres, under a court anti-trust decree, are not required to be licensed for ASCAP music. For a further discussion of the functions of the Harry Fox Office reference may be made to *This Business of Music.**

As in the case of popular music, the serious music composer under music industry standards will contract with the contracting ("original") publisher to receive 50 per cent of the mechanical-license and synchronization-license fees collected by the original publisher. Inasmuch as foreign subpublishers ordinarily retain 50 per cent of the mechanical-license and synchronization-license fees collected by them, remitting only the balance to the original publisher, the composer can expect to be paid one-quarter of the collections by the foreign subpublisher.

ASCAP

ASCAP and BMI have recognized that serious music composers are a cultural asset and should receive special consideration over and above the number of logged performances of their works. Composer Virgil Thomson has said that both ASCAP and BMI "have found they need the intellectual support, the prestige, of the serious composer, and have now come round to collecting and distributing in quite impressive amounts performance fees for serious music." He has paid tribute on behalf of the serious composers "to the composers of light music that we get paid at all for our performing rights, since it is they who have always organized the society for exacting such payment and furnished the funds for fighting infringers in the courts."

Stanley Adams, President of ASCAP, has said that ASCAP "has long recognized the importance of symphonic and concert works to the culture of the nation, and the Society's duty to encourage the creation of symphonic and concert works and to help ensure that the public will have continued access to them. In keeping with this objective, the Society adopted rules providing for additional credit for performances of serious works in symphony and concert halls."

MULTIPLE CREDITS

Until recently, the Society provided in substance for the distribution for performances of serious works in symphony and concert halls of 15 times the amount which the Society received for those performances. Having undertaken an effective campaign of educating the users of seri-

* Sidney Shemel and M. William Krasilovsky (New York, 1964) pp. 80, 106, 125-129, 164.

ous works to obtain licenses to perform the compositions, the Society noted that it had added many new licensees. The license fees paid by old and new licensees climbed to the point of a substantial increase in the distributions to writers of serious music. The Society therefore has placed a maximum limitation on added credit provisions which the Society applies to the amounts received for performances of serious works in symphony and concert halls.

ASCAP also uses multiple credits in connection with loggings of performances of serious works of 4 minutes or longer duration. The ASCAP Credit Weighting Formula calls for multiple credits in relation to the minutes of actual performance. For example, for a 5-minute performance, the multiple is 2; for a 10-minute performance, 5; for a 20-minute performance, 14; a 40-minute performance has a multiple of 44 and a 60-minute performance a multiple of 76. Performances on national radio network sustaining programs consisting of concerts by symphony orchestras which are presented as a genuine contribution to the culture of the nation are awarded credit equal to performances on a radio network of 50 stations.

There are included as Appendix H1 extracts from the ASCAP Credit Weighting Formula with respect to credit for performances of serious works. Appendix H2 contains examples of the limitations on added credit under Paragraph (H) of the ASCAP Credit Weighting Formula regarding concert and symphony hall performances.

QUALIFYING WORKS

ASCAP favors serious works in another respect. The Credit Weighting Formula provides that for works which in their original form were composed for a choral, symphonic or similar concert performance credits required to classify such a work as a "qualifying work" shall be reduced to 20 per cent of the number of feature performances required for other musical compositions. Under the "qualifying work" concept applied in the ASCAP system of credits, a popular song with a history of over 20,000 feature performances, of which the most recent five years contributed an aggregate of at least 2,500 feature performances, is given special higher credits when used in non-feature roles such as background, cue, bridge or theme; not more than 750 feature performances are to be counted in any one of the five years to meet the 2,500 requirement. There is also a partial qualification for higher credits if a work which passes the five year test has accumulated 15,000 or 10,000 feature performance credits.

Although a qualifying work employed as a theme is accorded half a feature credit, an unqualified work in the same form is granted only one-tenth of a feature credit. Half a feature credit is given to any background use, regardless of duration, of a qualifying work, while an unqualified work requires a 3-minute use for one-fourth of a feature credit, with reduction for lesser use. For example, a 20-second use of an unqualified work would earn only one-twentieth of a feature credit. As noted previously, serious works will be regarded as qualifying works although they log only 20 per cent of the number of feature performances required of other compositions.

SPECIAL AWARDS

Further special consideration for composers of serious music is given by ASCAP in certain other respects. In the distribution of moneys collected for the performance of symphonic and concert works, ASCAP does not deduct any administrative expenses. This is unlike the treatment of popular music.

ASCAP has a Special Awards Committee which through its Popular-Production Panel makes special monetary awards to popular music composers, and through its Standard Awards Panel to composers of symphonic and concert music. The panels are composed of persons of standing who are not ASCAP members.

Applications for awards are filed by writers or by others on behalf of writers; the staff of ASCAP does not initiate applications. The awards go to writers whose works have a unique prestige value for which adequate compensation would not otherwise be received by such composers, and to writers whose works are performed substantially in media not surveyed by ASCAP.

For example, awards have been made to Gian-Carlo Menotti and to Samuel Barber for $1,500 each. The aggregate sums awarded, in excess of $500,000, amount to close to 5 per cent of the total distributable revenues for writer members of ASCAP. Approximately two-thirds of the awards go to writers of serious music.

While in popular music the highest award is $1,000, in the serious music field the highest award is $2,000. In 1965, a spokesman on behalf of the Standard Awards Panel stated that the awards give "special recognition to talented new composers whose creative contributions are just beginning to be felt, as well as to outstanding established writers who have had a significant influence on our musical culture." Appendix I sets forth an extract from the ASCAP Writers' Distribution Formula relating to special awards.

ASCAP sponsors concert music showcase auditions for composers of concert music. These are open to writers of instrumental, chamber and vocal music who wish to audition their works before an invited audience of publishers, concert managers, professional composers and others.

Even the Articles of Association of ASCAP are designed to encourage the writers and publishers of serious music. They provide that the Board of Directors of ASCAP shall consist of 24 directors, 12 of whom shall be writer members and 12 of whom shall be publisher members. At all times, three of such writer members shall be "standard" writer members and, at all times, three of such publisher members must be "standard" publishers.

BMI

BMI uses the multiple credit system in favoring the writers and publishers of serious music. Triple credits for each three minutes of a serious work are provided for both radio and television feature performances. This is in contrast to single credits usual for popular songs. However, for non-feature uses, multiple credits for serious music will not be applied.

BMI has for many years followed a program of fostering serious music. The full-time services of an expert have been and are employed to promote concert works. BMI has entered into agreements with an organization of about 135 serious composers known as the American Composers Alliance.

Under these agreements, composers whose music is channelled to BMI through the Alliance receive performance fees through the Alliance on a favorable guaranteed payment basis. The allocation of the fees is determined by the Alliance, using factors of "current performance," "accumulated eligibility," "availability of scores " and "sustained performance." The guarantee is in excess of the amounts which would be payable if only actual performances were considered. There is included as Appendix J the Alliance's form of assignment of performing rights to be executed by each member.

BMI also makes annual Student Composer Awards of money to promising Western Hemisphere composers. The sum of $7,500 a year is appropriated for this purpose.

PROMOTIONAL PUBLICATIONS

BMI, since 1951, has compiled and published a pamphlet entitled

"Concert Music USA." There have been 12 revised editions, up to the issue entitled "1966 Concert Music USA." The publication surveys in brief, and with emphasis on statistics of recent growth, activities of symphony orchestras, classical recordings, concert music, broadcasting, opera groups and music instruction.

Both BMI and ASCAP have separately issued a catalog of the serious music of their respective members or affiliates licensed through the performing rights organization.

Biographical profiles of its more prominent serious music composers are released from time to time by BMI. There is cooperation between BMI and the American Symphony Orchestra League in annual orchestra surveys.

It has been estimated that BMI spends about $1,000,000 a year in the sphere of serious music, for writer and publisher distributions and other activities.

OTHER PERFORMING RIGHT ASPECTS

It is customary for ASCAP and BMI publishers to negotiate directly the premiere concert performance of a serious music composition.

The ASCAP publishers arrange for an appropriate music score rental fee. Performance right licensing is handled by ASCAP. Under licenses issued by ASCAP to symphony orchestras and other non-broadcasting users of serious music, ASCAP is entitled to restrict the first United States performance of a composition. In that event, ASCAP acts on the publisher's request. It appears that ASCAP's practice of restricting the first performance until cleared by its publishers enables its publishers to negotiate appropriate terms for score rentals and other elements of the concert. Forms of the ASCAP symphony license applicable to community orchestras and of the ASCAP license for colleges and universities are included as Appendixes K and L respectively.

At the present time BMI publishers, in addition to renting the music score, license directly not only the premiere performance but also all other live performances as well. The theory of BMI at the present time is that its publishers will derive greater earnings from direct licensing than they would earn through logged performance fee payments for the premiere or other live performances collected through BMI.

It has been noted that certain publishers, especially in the symphonic field, tend to increase the rental fees for scores if a performance is intended to be broadcast. The greater fee for broadcast rights seems difficult to justify since radio and television stations appear to be covered by the blanket licenses issued by BMI and ASCAP.

Foreign performing right societies, as a rule, give extra weight to performances of serious music. Through their arrangements with foreign societies, ASCAP and BMI are able to collect from abroad for American members or affiliates. The writers and publishers of American serious music thereby benefit from the favorable weighting accorded to serious music performances by the foreign societies.

GRAND RIGHTS

Serious music composers who create music for dramatic productions will be interested in the distinction between dramatic performance rights (frequently called "grand rights"), and non-dramatic performance rights ("small rights"). Grand rights cover the dramatic renditions of operas, operettas, musical comedies, ballets, revues, sketches and like productions, in whole or in part.

A separate composition which does not originate in an opera or other dramatic production may also involve a grand right if it is woven into and carries forward the plot of a broadcasting program and its accompanying action.

ASCAP obtains from its members only non-dramatic small performance rights. BMI acquires the right to license dramatic performances of up to 30 minutes of selections from opera, operettas and musical comedies. While dramatic performance rights are included in its licenses to stations, BMI reserves the right to restrict dramatic uses in its clearance bulletins. BMI licenses to broadcasters also permit the dramatization of a non-dramatic individual song. The standard SESAC license excludes grand rights, which are licensed separately by SESAC. If the performing right organization does not license a dramatic performance, the prospective user must seek a license from the publisher or from the writer if he has reserved the dramatic right.

PRINTED EDITIONS

In the case of an opera, a printed edition means a vocal score. As to other works, there will be a full score in a large edition, or a pocket-size study edition. Costs for the copying and other preparation may vary from $1,500 to $10,000, with many major works falling in the $5,000 to $6,000 range. The high cost of copying in the United States has led to the referral of a considerable amount of such work to lower-cost European and Asian experts. Many a contemporary composer becomes his own copyist in order to encourage the printing and performance of his work.

Particularly in regard to new music, it becomes difficult to justify on a purely business basis the expense of launching printed editions of serious works. The Rockefeller Panel Report on The Performing Arts was moved to state (p. 104):

> ". . . a review is required of the entire system of publishing and distributing new music. As economic patterns have changed, this can no longer be done adequately by publishers, commercial or nonprofit, without some form of outside assistance."

A printed opera vocal score will be priced from $5 to $9.50 or even higher, with comparable prices for symphony scores. Obviously, there are few prospective purchasers. Rentals, rather than purchases, of parts have tended to become the prevailing practice. In addition, the publisher charges a dramatic performance fee for the performance of the opera. With respect to minor works frequently performed at schools, the rental price of the opera score may include the performance fee. ASCAP and BMI, as noted previously, do not license dramatic performance rights of dramatic works.

MUSIC SALES ROYALTIES

For sales of serious music editions in the United States and Canada, the standard royalty payable to the composer is 10 per cent of the suggested retail list prices established by the publisher. This may be contrasted with a usual royalty for popular music approximating 10 per cent of the wholesale price. Some representatives of serious music composers contend that the royalty should be a minimum of 12½ per cent of the suggested retail price, and should increase to not less than 15 per cent after a stipulated number of sales.

The composer will be entitled to receive 50 per cent of the receipts of the publisher from sales of printed editions through subpublishers outside the United States and Canada. The publisher usually is paid 10 per cent of the suggested retail list prices in the foreign countries.

RENTAL INCOME

With regard to the publishers' income from rentals, the share of such rentals payable to the composer will frequently depend on whether the publisher or the composer pays the expense of extraction and preparation of parts on master sheets. This may run from $5,000 to $6,000 for a major work. If the publisher pays the expense, the composer commonly receives 25 per cent of the rental income. In the event the expense is borne by the composer, his share is likely to be 50 per cent of the rental income. Composers may contend that rental payments to them should never be less than 50 per cent irrespective of whether the composer or the publisher bears the expense of extraction and preparation of parts.

One of the advantages to the publisher of rentals, as opposed to sales, is that the publisher may achieve a greater voice in selecting the performers of the work, and avoiding poorly timed competing performances. For frequently played scores, it is not unusual to have 15 to 20 rental sets in use at any one time. For example, Aaron Copland's "Lincoln Portrait" is the subject of many rentals.

PRINTING

The printing of a serious work is of pre-eminent importance in the obtaining of performances and recordings of the work.

An important problem of the serious music composer is the contractual obligations of publishers as to printing and rentals. The writer will wish to ensure that his work is printed and made available for sale to the public. Because of the expense of printing and the thinness of the prospective market, the publisher may avoid a firm commitment to print. This is a subject for bargaining between the composer and publisher. They may compromise by providing that all rights will revert to the composer if the publisher fails to print within a stipulated period, such as one year after the first performance.

A publisher, although averse to a printing commitment, may agree to provide rental copies. These are often ozalid reproductions from transparencies originally prepared by the composer. The cost to the publisher is considerably less than the expense of printing. Composers may be dissatisfied with only rental copies since they are relatively few in number and the public will be unable to purchase copies of the serious music work. In the absence of printed editions, copies are generally unavailable to amateurs, and promotional distribution to encourage performances and recordings is restricted.

PROSPECTS FOR NEW WORKS

A characteristic of the opera world is its adherence to the standard works, the established performers and the accepted style of presentation.

Relatively few contemporary works are presented by the renowned opera companies. Together with the emphasis by symphony orchestras and many performers on traditional repertoire, it can be easily seen that the opportunities for contemporary composers and enterprising new publishers in the field of serious music tend to be limited.

It has been said that the business of publishing new serious works rivals the new Broadway stage productions in the risks involved. Demand must be generated from a public which appears generally unwilling to buy enough records to warrant commercial recordings of new works. Orchestras which operate at serious deficits and have limited funds for rehearsals are loath to incur the expense and risk in sponsoring new works.

The need to subsidize contemporary composition has been recognized by various groups. Certain foundations have paid the recording costs for phonograph records of new compositions. Orchestras and opera groups associated with colleges and universities and supported by educational funds have assumed a commanding position in performing new works. BMI's annual guarantees to serious music publishers, and to writers through the American Composers Alliance, are in effect a form of subsidy of serious works, as are the multiple credits applied by ASCAP and BMI in evaluating serious music performances.

AMERICAN COMPOSERS ALLIANCE

Cooperative and self-help ventures by composers are a feature of the serious music field. The American Composers Alliance ("ACA") acts as a publisher for its members in its Composers Facsimile Edition operation, which arranges for the reproduction of its members' material when a purchase order is received. The reproduction is by the ozalid process from transparencies prepared by the composers as they composed.

ACA, in addition, conducts a loan library of its members' works, including parts to be performed by musicians, making loans for one month without charge. ACA acts for its members in handling synchronization licenses for films and mechanical licenses for records, and in licensing the live concerts of their works and collecting rental fees for scores in connection with the concerts; the entire proceeds are paid to the particular member.

COMPOSERS RECORDINGS, INC.

ACA is active in the recording of contemporary American music through Composers Recordings, Inc. ("CRI"). A majority interest in CRI is owned by ACA, and a minority by foundation-originated American Musical Associates. CRI is headquartered at ACA.

CRI produces and distributes many recordings of contemporary American works, most of which have not been previously recorded. The CRI 1966 catalog lists 110 LP's on which more than 320 titles are represented. The limitations of the CRI recording budget are indicated by the fact that orchestral works have been recorded predominantly outside the United States by lower-cost orchestras in countries such as Japan, Norway, England and Italy.

Among the relatively few American orchestras recorded are Leopold Stokowski and his orchestra and the San Francisco, Knoxville and Oklahoma City symphony orchestras. Often recordings are made after a work has been rehearsed thoroughly for a live concert, thus causing a substantial saving of rehearsal expenses otherwise required for recordings.

The recording budget of CRI is derived from three main sources. More than half is received from private foundations and individuals. The balance is obtained in the main from ACA and also from the American Academy of Arts and Letters which selects four young composers each year to be recorded. Both ACA writers and non-ACA writers are represented in the recordings, and ASCAP, BMI and non-affiliated music is contained in the records. A committee of distinguished musicians passes on all recording projects. CRI recordings are distributed by mail and through record distributors.

AMERICAN MUSIC CENTER

The American Music Center, Inc., which has been designated as the official United States Information Center for Music, was founded in 1940 and is a non-profit organization of over 500 composer members and 200 other members, including publishers. It maintains the world's largest circulating library of serious American music, available to conductors, performers, teachers, students and others, on loan, without charge, for 30 days.

The scores library, which does not include parts to be performed by musicians, contained in excess of 9,000 works in 1965. Many of the scores would be otherwise unavailable. The composer members receive discounts on reproduction services, on recording services and on purchases of scores, books, music and records. The organization receives its support from membership dues and from grants by foundations and others.

Independent of the American Composers Alliance and the American

Music Center is the New Music Edition Society. This Society was orig-inally organized by the late Henry Cowell, the well-known serious music composer who was also active in the American Composers Alliance. It aids the publication of new works of serious music composers. The Society publishes under the aegis of the Theodore Presser Company of Bryn Mawr, Pennsylvania. It issues the new works recommended by the Society on an irregular basis, and as a "new issue" distributed to music stores and other Theodore Presser outlets.

SPECIAL GRANTS

In 1965, the Ford Foundation announced grants and endowment funds totalling $85 million to be given to about 50 symphony orchestras throughout the United States. The orchestras must raise matching funds, except for $21 million. The matchable $64 million will be granted to a trust fund, the annual income of which will be distributed to the orchestras. After 10 years, the trust fund will be liquidated and the money apportioned to the orchestras.

The orchestras can use the money as they see fit, such as for salaries, lengthening seasons and hiring soloists, etc. It may be anticipated that the funds will have a beneficial effect in encouraging the performance of new works.

This result is also expected from the new program of the United States government in its National Endowment for the Arts. Grants to individual creative writers are an integral part of the Federal subsidy.

Writers receive further encouragement through music fellowships and grants sponsored by private foundations and funds, including those established in the names of Ford, Guggenheim, Fromm, Koussevitzky, Martha Baird Rockefeller and Naumberg.

COMMISSIONED WORKS

Just as Frederick the Great subsidized composers of his day, we find foundations, corporations and individuals commissioning concert works today. This granting of commissions to composers for new works is a distinctive characteristic of the field of serious music.

A commission involves several aspects. The composer agrees to write a specific work or type of work. The commissioning party undertakes to make a payment to the composer, or to guarantee a concert performance, or both. In fact, the assurance of a first performance may often be more attractive to the composer than a payment, and will be a decided factor in negotiations as to the amount of the payment.

The consideration to the commissioning party frequently entails the dedication of the piece to the patron. If the patron is a performer, he may be granted the exclusive rights to perform and/or record the new work, not only for the premiere performance but also for a period of years. Rarely will the patron reserve the right to designate the publisher of the piece.

A question may arise as to whether the patron or the composer is vested with the ownership of the copyright in a commissioned work. The parties may contract freely in this regard. The foundation, philanthropist or performer acting as patron may be expected to have no interest in the copyright proprietorship. But a serious music publisher who is a patron may seek the copyright ownership, subject to the payment of writer royalties.

Under customs and usages applicable to commissioned serious music works, in the absence of a definitive agreement, a composer is regarded as an independent contractor, rather than an employee-for-hire, and is deemed to be the copyright proprietor.

A commission is considered to be an honor to the composer of serious music, worthy of mention along with references to the winning of contest prizes, fellowships and awards.

COMPOSER EARNINGS

Serious music composers, as is the case with serious musicians, are in the main unable to support themselves from the proceeds of their work as writers. Referring to the increased performance fees for serious music paid by ASCAP, and by BMI, Composer Virgil Thomson wrote in 1961: "As a result, and also as a result of enlarged foundational patronage, today's young composers get commissioned, paid, played and even published. They are not yet living on their take; only five standard composers in America can do that. The rest still teach, mostly in universities. But they are better off than their European confreres, who are paid less for their teaching."

In 1960, Aaron Copland, describing Dr. Serge Koussevitzky, leader of the Boston Symphony Orchestra, wrote: "He has been profoundly disturbed at the realization that the great majority of our composers devote the major part of their time, not to writing music, but to the gaining of a livelihood. He can never accustom himself to the thought that in this rich country of ours no plan exists that would provide composers with a modicum of financial security for the production of works of serious music."

The better climate of governmental subsidies in the United States has been previously referred to at pages 3-4. Recognition by ASCAP and BMI of the need to subsidize serious music composers has been discussed heretofore more fully at pages 28-33 and 36.

The *ASCAP News,* from time to time, lists current contests in which serious music composers are entitled to compete. For example, in 1965 there was a reference to a Puccini Opera Competition sponsored by Boston University's School of Fine and Applied Arts, wherein a chamber music work by a United States citizen under 35 years of age, would be entered for a prize of $500 and a round trip to, and a performance at, the Festival of Two Worlds, at Spoleto, Italy.

Other contests were for three separate Prince Rainier III of Monaco Music Prizes of 5,000 French francs, 10,000 French francs, and 30,000 French francs, respectively, for a chamber music work, an orchestral piece, and a scenic (notably opera or ballet) musical work. There was an $8,000 prize for a new opera on which La Scala would take a one year option for the first performance.

A list and description of foundations, trusts and other sources of funds for grants and awards for music, as well as of schools offering graduate fellowships and scholarships in music, may be obtained from The Music Educators National Conference, The National Education Association, 1202 Sixteenth Street, N.W., Washington 6, D.C. Another source is the annual edition of *Musical America.*

PART TWO

OTHER ASPECTS OF THE MUSIC INDUSTRY

5

PRODUCTION AND SALE OF PRINTED MUSIC

UPON his appointment to the United States Supreme Court, attention was called to the musical habits of Justice Abe Fortas. One evening a week, regularly, he joins with three other musicians in performing privately as a string quartet. In doing so, he is one of 37 million Americans who are in the amateur category. This is defined by the American Music Conference as comprising persons who play non-professionally six or more times a year. Twelve million of these amateurs are of school age. There were, in 1965, 22 million piano players, a figure that rose 12 per cent in the past decade; 7½ million guitarists, a category of rapid growth; over 3½ million organists; and numerous woodwind instrumentalists.

The boom in instrument sales was recognized by the Columbia Broadcasting System in its 1965 acquisition for $13 million of the Fender Guitar and Amplifier Corporation, a manufacturer of electric guitars and amplifiers. Commenting on the purchase, Goddard Leiberson, president of Columbia Records, said:

> "This is a fast-growing business tied into the expanding leisure time market. We expect this industry will grow by 23 per cent in the next two years."

The number of instrumentalists and of instruments in the hands of the public are reflected in the sales and uses of printed music.

TYPES OF PRINTED MUSIC

The same composition may be available for use in many different printed versions. There are numerous printed editions of the single selection, "Rhapsody in Blue," ranging from a full symphonic orchestra score with a list price of $37.50, to a guitar solo of the theme selling for 50 cents. A piece that is available in a wide range of individual printed forms will appear in folios, which are soft-cover collections, and in song books or albums. These may have a list price as high as $10 for the hard-cover illustrated edition. Examples of the types of printed music available are shown in the following list:

ACCORDION
Band
Collections and Methods

BAND
Collections (Folios)
Concert Selections (Octavo Size)
Concert Selections (Quarto Size)
Methods
Quickstep Size

BRASS
Solos, Duets, Trio and Ensembles

CANTATAS AND CHORAL ARRANGEMENTS
Unison
Two Part
SSA (Soprano, Soprano and Alto)
SSAA (Soprano, Soprano, Alto and Alto)
SATB (Soprano, Alto, Tenor and Bass)
Three Part Male
TTBB (Tenor, Tenor, Bass and Bass)
Multiple Choirs
Choral Collections
Choral Selections
Festival Choral Works

DANCE ORCHESTRA
Collections (Folios)
Series
School Stage Band Series
Standard Stock Arrangements

FRETTED INSTRUMENTS
Collections and Methods
Solos

HARMONICA COLLECTIONS

METHODS AND STUDIES
Instrumental
Strings
Band and Orchestra

ORCHESTRA
Collections (Folios)
Concert Selections
Major Orchestral Works
Miniature Scores (Full)
String Orchestra
String Orchestra Collections

ORGAN
Methods
Collections
Solos
Duets (Organ & Piano)

PERCUSSION

PIANO
Methods and Studies
Collections (Folios)
Teaching and Recital Pieces
Piano Duets
Two Pianos — Four Hands
Solos

STRINGS
Banjo
Guitar
Mandolin
Baritone Ukelele
Ukelele
Violin
Viola
Methods

Solos and Duets
Trios and Quartets

VOCAL
Collections (Song) (Folios)
Community Song Books (Lyrics)
Duets, Secular & Sacred
Duet Collections (Folios)
Folk Collections (Folios)
Methods
Pocket Size Song Books
Scores
Selections
Songs, Standard, Sacred & Popular
Song Books (Cloth Bound,
     with Music)

"Educational music" is music intended to be sold to schools, colleges, institutions or industrial plants for performances by amateur musical groups. Included are solo or group arrangements of classical, semi-classical and popular music deemed suitable for vocal or instrumental renditions.

For example, there are educational versions of "Begin The Beguine" and "Smoke Gets In Your Eyes." To meet the demand for multiple voice and instrument combinations, the number of different publications of the same song may exceed 50 or more. Arrangements of popular music are often revised to satisfy the most recent taste of the public. Classical and semi-classical music arrangements are modified from time to time to include different instrumentation and voices.

INDEXES TO PRINTED MUSIC

Some of the indexes available to printed music are listed in Appendix Q to *This Business of Music.** Others are set forth in the "Guide Books of Publications" list prepared by the Music Publishers' Association of the United States, Inc. of 609 Fifth Ave., New York, New York, and contained in its free booklet entitled "How to Improve Your Sheet Music Business." The tremendous amount of printed music now outstanding is indicated by the fact that band music alone, published in the United States, constitutes over 16,000 titles, and separate choral music indexes are required for schools, churches and funerals.

* Sidney Shemel and M. William Krasilovsky (New York, 1964) p. 317.

FAKE BOOKS

A major problem in the field of printed music is the illegal publication of popular song collections. These are in large demand, especially by professional dance bands.

A fake book is an illegal unauthorized compilation of the melody line and chord symbols of as many as 1,000 top songs. It is sold for varying prices ranging as high as $35.00. It flouts the Copyright Act, which gives to the copyright proprietor the exclusive right to make and print copies of compositions.

The illegal printer and distributor pay no royalties to the legal composers and publishers of songs contained in the fake book. In effect, the fake book replaces and substitutes for folios and sheet music, on the sales of which writers would earn royalties and publishers would derive profits.

Assuming a retail price of 75 cents for a copy of sheet music of a popular song, the sheet music for 1,000 such songs in a fake book would sell for an aggregate of $750.00. Instead the fake book may sell for $35.00.

The bargain price to the user and the profit to the illicit printer and distributor make fake books difficult to control. Substantial awards of damages under the Copyright Act have been made by courts against fake book printers and distributors, and the dealer of such books is also liable.

Moreover, criminal penalties under Section 104 of the Copyright Act are available. These are sought by the National Music Publishers' Association, Inc., of 460 Park Avenue, New York, New York, against persons who willfully and for profit engage in the printing or selling of fake books, or knowingly and willfully aid or abet such infringement. The practice constitutes a misdemeanor punishable by imprisonment of up to one year, or by a fine of from $100 to $1,000, or both. A copy of Section 104 of the Copyright Act is included as Appendix M.

Acting under the criminal provisions of the Copyright Act, in 1966 a Federal jury in New York convicted a Long Island band leader for publishing fake books without paying royalties to the copyright owners. He allegedly published more than 46,000 plastic-bound books which included songs by, among others, George Gershwin, Lorenz Hart and Oscar Hammerstein. According to the United States Attorney the $35.00 book was to return $1.6 million on an investment of $81,535.

Acting to combat fake books, a number of larger publishers and some of the independent licensee distributors of printed editions have published legitimate compilations of numerous songs in the same form as fake books. These are sold for prices ranging up to about $10.00.

PREPARATION FOR PRINTING

Rarely in any field of music does a composer submit a manuscript that is ready for printing.

Popular songs accepted by a publisher from a writer are usually in lead sheet form which requires arrangement and copying in preparation for printing. For folk and rock and roll music, lead sheets are often not submitted, and it is necessary for the publisher to engage a skilled copyist to write a lead sheet on the basis of listening to a phonograph recording.

Arrangements are made by staff arrangers in the case of several major publishers, or by free lance arrangers who are paid fees for their services. Staff or free lance personnel then take over, operating either by hand or by a music typewriter, in preparation for photo-offset printing.

In the serious music field, the composer's basic manuscript requires substantial copying services and costs to ready the many orchestral parts for printing.

Attractive packaging has become a significant factor in achieving sales of printed editions. Folios and current hit sheet music copies are deemed to require appealing artwork for covers and color printing in order to compete in the impulse-buying market. Color is often essential to make a folio or other publication stand out on a music store rack. Some covers are printed in four colors.

Most publishers use independent printers who can offer the speed, efficiency and economies of modern giant presses, as well as color printing.

ROYALTIES

The writer contracts in the popular music field set forth royalties payable for various categories of printed editions. The rate for sheet music usually ranges between 3 cents and 6 cents. Many publishers pay 6 cents for show tunes or, in contracts negotiated for the renewal period of the United States copyright, for established standards. Slightly less is paid for motion picture themes, and the lowest royalty is applied to new popular songs.

Some royalty contracts, including an alternate provision in the 1947 Uniform Popular Songwriters Contract promulgated by the American Guild of Authors and Composers ("AGAC"), contain sliding scales of sheet music royalties. These range up to 23 per cent of the wholesale price on copies sold in excess of 500,000. This sliding scale provision is rarely used, however. It involves cumbersome bookkeeping, and usually an unrealistic idea of anticipated sales.

While there are exceptions for top hits, sheet music sales of most rock and roll compositions are small. For many songs, the sales are less than the minimum printing order of 1,000 copies. Many popular songs, especially rock and roll, are never printed.

Individual popular songs are rarely printed in any form other than piano-vocal sheet music or in folios until they become accepted as standard hits.

As a rule, the royalty for orchestrations, band arrangements, octavos, quartets, combinations of voices and instruments, and other copies of songs is 10 per cent of the wholesale selling price. Oddly enough, many popular publisher-songwriter contracts inadvertently base royalties on the retail price rather than on the wholesale price which is the standard for even the writer-oriented contract form of AGAC.

When a song is included in a folio or other collection, the AGAC contract and many other contracts provide that the aggregate royalty of 10 per cent of the wholesale selling price is prorated among all the copyrighted songs in the compilation. Thus, in a folio of 10 copyrighted songs, 1 per cent is applied to each song. If additional public domain songs are included in the folio, there is no diminution of the royalty of each copyrighted composition.

In the contract forms of some publishers no distinction is made between copyrighted and public domain songs in determining the prorated royalty. This results in a lower percentage royalty for each copyrighted song. However, the wholesale selling price on which the percentage is computed may be increased by the inclusion of the public domain songs in the compilation. When more than 25 songs are included in a folio, the overall rate is increased under the AGAC contract and under many other contracts, by an additional ½ per cent for each composition over 25.

INDEPENDENT FOLIO LICENSEES AND SELLING AGENTS

In today's popular market, a large percentage of folios are not prepared and issued by the publishers of the compositions. Many publishers, especially the smaller ones without extensive catalogs, utilize the services of independent folio publishers and distributors, such as Hansen Publications, Inc., Plymouth Music Co., Inc. and Cimino Publications, Inc. These arrangements may be either exclusive or non-exclusive.

In the relationship between the music publisher and the folio publisher the latter is usually either a licensee or a selling agent. Generally, a licensee arrangement provides for payment to the music publisher of a stated royalty. The folio publisher bears all costs of preparation and printing, and the risks of unsold inventory.

Under a selling agency, the music publisher pays the expense of preparation and printing, and is entitled to the sales receipts less a commission to the agent. There are elements common to both licensees and selling agents. The folio distributor, in both instances, handles the production and printing for the music publisher, and the sales organization of the folio distributor is utilized. Billing to dealers may also be similar.

The variance in the arrangements can result in a difference in the royalties payable to songwriters. In the case of a folio license, under many songwriter agreements, the publisher's United States and Canadian royalties are shared with songwriters on a pro rata basis. The AGAC form of agreement fixes the writer's share as 50 per cent.

In the event of a selling agency, the songwriter royalty under the AGAC contract and under many agreements would be the same as that for folios handled directly in the United States and Canada by the music publisher, namely, a pro rata portion of 10 per cent of the wholesale selling price.

Most popular music folios are issued by independent folio distributors acting as licensees. The licensee method has proved to be most adaptable to combining the songs of diverse publishers in one publication. Such compilations are generally found to achieve the greatest appeal to the retail buying public.

Under the AGAC contract, immediate licensing to independent licensees is permitted for lyrics. However, lyrics and music in combination may not be licensed for song books, song sheets, folios, or similar combinations containing at least four compositions, for a period of two years from the original publication date of regular piano copies. This may be harmful to the publisher and the writer if the latter is not available to approve (or if he disapproves) the licensing to an independent licensee-distributor of current hits which may have only a short popular life.

FOLIO LICENSEE ROYALTIES

What royalties are paid by independent folio distributor-licensees to music publishers? Typical rates are as follows for folio and other editions, other than regular sheet music:

10 per cent of the retail selling price for dance orchestration, stage dance band, concert or marching band editions;

20 per cent of the retail selling price for instrumental, accordion, guitar or organ solo editions, and choral editions;

a pro rata portion of 10 per cent of the retail selling price for folio, book or other collections.

Royalties to the licensor-publisher on the above editions are customarily paid on the number of copies printed, rather than those sold. In addition, there is an allowance of 10 per cent of the number printed to cover returns, damaged copies, etc. A typical contract form of license for folio and other editions is included as Appendix N.

FOLIO SELLING AGENT COMMISSIONS

As previously noted, folios are also issued through selling agents. They are paid a commission for their services, with the costs of printing and preparation of editions borne by the music publisher. The commissions charged may vary from about 15 to 20 per cent of the amounts received from sales.

SHEET MUSIC LICENSEES

The same independent folio distributors, in addition, serve music publishers in the more volatile business of printing and selling regular piano-vocal copies. As many as 75,000 to 100,000 copies of a top hit can be sold in a year. Other songs may not even sell their minimum printing orders. Here, too, there are licensee and selling agency arrangements made with music publishers.

Under one licensee form of agreement the distributor pays all expenses of preparation and production of copies. However, instead of the percentage royalties payable on folio editions, such as 10 per cent of the retail price on sales, there is a payment to the music publisher of 20 or 25 cents per copy in relation to sales.

On sales made to dealers with a right to return unsold copies, there are monthly sales reports, while accountings are rendered to the publisher 30 or more days (90 days is not uncommon) after the final returnable date. After such date, sales are made on non-returnable terms, and accountings are rendered either on the number printed or in inventory, or in certain instances on those sold. Accountings and payments for non-returnable sales are commonly made on a quarterly basis.

Sometimes the distributor will pay an advance to the publisher, recoupable out of the royalties on sales. A form of contract covering a licensee arrangement for sheet music is set forth as Appendix O.

In a variation of the licensee agreement, one large distributor pays 20 cents per piano-vocal copy on 90 per cent of print orders, less free promotional copies and excess copies which are destroyed. This distributor previously paid 25 cents per piano-vocal copy on all sales.

It contends that the lower rate is required by newly instituted higher-cost intensified direct selling to jobbers and dealers by in-person and telephone contacts. According to the distributor, greater sales result therefrom. The same distributor has discontinued making new selling agency arrangements.

SHEET MUSIC SELLING AGENCY

Some distributors also offer to act as selling agents, as an alternative to being licensees, for sheet music distribution. In this field, the selling agent may charge a fee of about $15 for the use of its production facilities, plus the actual costs of production including engraving, artwork, type and printing.

As noted previously, the receipts from sales are paid to the music publisher less the agent's commissions which, as in the case of folio editions, are in a range of 15 to 20 per cent of receipts. A form of a selling agent contract for sheet music is included as Appendix P.

Emphasizing its role as agent rather than a licensee, one firm offers special procedures for exclusive selling agent rights to an entire catalog for a period of years. All bills for printing by outside printers are rendered, and all sales invoices are issued in the name of the song publisher at the address of the sales agent.

Checks from jobbers and dealers in payment for printed editions are drawn directly to the order of the song publisher, and these checks are transmitted monthly to the song publisher with statements showing the number of copies sold. The agent's commission of 15 per cent is billed monthly to the song publisher.

These procedures give added assurance to the song publisher that bills for printing and receipts from sales are proper. They also help to establish and preserve customer relations between the song publisher and the jobber or dealer. A form of contract for this type of selling agent arrangement is set forth as Appendix Q.

TERM OF LICENSEE OR SELLING AGENT AGREEMENTS

The minimum terms of the non-exclusive or exclusive licensee or sales agent agreements range from one to five years. The contracts frequently provide for automatic extensions from year to year, unless either party gives a written notice of termination prior to the anniversary date. A licensee-distributor ordinarily will be granted the right to sell off accumulated inventory on hand at the termination date, subject to its rendering statements and paying royalties in accordance with the agreement between the parties. As to selling agencies, there may be a provision for return or destruction of the inventory at the termination date.

LYRIC LICENSES

Song lyric publications seek licenses from publishers to print and vend the lyrics of hit popular songs. Licenses are sought for the United States and Canada, generally for a period of one year. Flat payments are made for the licenses, rather than royalties. For the usual song hit, the payment will approximate $75.00. It is often provided that if the song achieves one of the top ten positions in the *Billboard* chart of top hits, an additional sum of, say, $50.00 will be paid. There is set forth as Appendix R a form of license agreement for lyric reprint rights.

COPYRIGHT NOTICE

To avoid dedication of a work to the public, the publication of the work must include a notice of copyright on each copy sold or offered for sale or publicly distributed. It is, therefore, imperative that a provision requiring a notice of copyright be inserted in licensee and selling agent agreements.

A common clause states that the licensee or selling agent will include a notice of copyright on each copy of the printed edition. The same provision sets forth the exact form of notice, or a model form of notice, or stipulates that the copyright owner will prescribe the form of notice to be followed.

Under Paragraph 19 of the Copyright Act of the United States, a notice of copyright shall consist of the symbol © or the word "Copyright," or the abbreviation "Copr.," together with the copyright proprietor's name. With respect to printed, literary, musical or dramatic works, the year of first publication is also stated.

A typical form of notice is:

© John Doe 1966 or Copyright 1966 by John Doe

For works previously registered for copyright in unpublished form, the notice should contain the year date of registration for the unpublished version, instead of the year of first publication. If the published version includes new copyrightable matter, it is advisable that both the year date of registration as an unpublished work and the year date of publication be included.

With regard to musical works, the Copyright Act provides that the notice must appear upon the title page, or first page of the music.

The United States and over 50 other countries adhere to the Universal Copyright Convention. For reciprocal international protection of a work in these countries pursuant to the Convention, the required notice of copyright consists of the symbol ©, accompanied by the name of the copyright owner and the year date of publication. An example is:

© John Doe 1966

This form of notice, as indicated previously, also qualifies under Paragraph 19 of the United States Copyright Act.

Many publishers will also attempt to obtain reciprocal international copyright protection in the many countries which adhere to the Berne Convention, and in the Western Hemisphere nations which are parties to the Buenos Aires Convention of 1910. The United States is a signatory to the latter, but not the former, convention.

A work originating in a non-Berne Convention country such as the United States will be afforded protection under that convention if published first or simultaneously in a country which has signed the convention. American publishers who seek Berne Convention protection will usually arrange for first or simultaneous publication in Canada or England which adhere to the convention.

The Buenos Aires Convention calls for each work to carry a notice that property rights in a copyright are reserved. While the United States form of copyright notice seems sufficient for this purpose, it appears advisable to add the words "All Rights Reserved" to the copyright notice to ensure protection under the Buenos Aires Convention.

Independent licensee-distributors or selling agents for printed editions can usually be helpful in advising and arranging for proper copyright notices, and for simultaneous publication in a Berne Convention country.

For a further discussion of notices and other formalities, including registration and deposit, involved in copyright protection in the United States and elsewhere, reference may be made to chapters entitled "The

Nature of Copyright in The United States" and "International Copyright Protection" contained in *This Business Of Music.**

RETURN PRIVILEGES

Return privileges to jobbers or dealers mean that they may return unsold copies to the seller. Such privileges are a means for encouraging them to stock copies without risk until they have a full opportunity to promote and sell the copies.

Often a song will be on the popular hit charts for only four to five weeks, and sheet music of the song will not sell thereafter. Return privileges may ensure that the jobber or dealer will stock sufficient copies to satisfy the public demand during the peak popularity of the song.

The short span and the volatility of the popular piano-vocal sheet music market make the risk of returnable jobber or dealer inventory a matter of considerable concern to the distributors. One major distributor reduces its risk by giving special discounts to jobbers or dealers who accept large quantities of printed copies without return privileges.

Popular song copies are usually sold with a full returnable privilege unless a special discount deal has been arranged. Show tune sheet music is in some cases fully returnable and in others non-returnable from its inception.

DISCOUNTS

The basic discount structure for sales on daily orders rather than by stock orders provides for a jobber to receive discounts of from 33⅓ to 50 per cent of the retail price, and for discounts to dealers of from 25 to 40 per cent of the retail price. The lowest rates are for symphonic scores. The highest rates are for popular music.

Stock order discounts are higher, ranging from 50 plus 10 per cent to 60 per cent to jobbers, and from 40 plus 10 per cent to 50 plus 10 per cent to dealers. A 50 plus 10 per cent discount means there is a basic discount of 50 per cent from the retail price, resulting in 37.5 cents on a 75-cent item. In addition, 10 per cent more on the discounted price, or 3.75 cents, is further deducted from the retail price.

A stock order purchase means that the dealer, using the individual publisher or distributor's catalog or stock order bulletin, forwards semi-annual orders in bulk rather than on a daily hit or miss basis. Stock orders are gauged to meet the store's six month requirements.

* Sidney Shemel and M. William Krasilovsky (New York, 1964) pp. 63, 81.

As noted previously, there is a variation in dealer discounts. While some publishers determine a retail store's daily order discount standing by the volume of daily orders in particular categories of music (such as show, popular, band, folk, concert, etc.), it is common for a store's discount status to depend on the volume and regularity of its stock order purchases in the specific music categories. The discount status applies to the particular kind of music, such as folk music, rather than to the store as a whole.

Discount ratings also depend on the dealer's willingness to buy and display "new issues" in the categories involved. A new issue is a new printed edition, for which special incentive discounts are offered in return for the dealer's purchases, without viewing a sample. A new issue discount will often be an extra 10 per cent off the normal discounted figure. Frequently, there may be one reorder within a limited time at the same new issue discount.

Whereas most publishers may offer no discount on direct sales of educational music to institutions, some may offer discounts of from 10 to 15 per cent depending on the potential buying capacity of the institution. Jobbers and dealers selling educational music may grant varying discounts in order to encourage sales.

PRICES OF PRINTED MUSIC

A copy of piano-vocal sheet music usually sells for 75 cents and it costs the publisher less than 10 cents to print in quantities of 1,000 or more copies. A $1.95 folio of ten or twelve songs can be printed in quantity for about 30 cents. A symphonic study score may sell for about $5.00, and a full symphonic orchestration of a major piece for as much as $40.00; for the limited quantities expected to be sold, the printing costs can exceed the selling price.

The publisher's operating expenses generally exceed his printing costs. Apart from being influenced by overhead costs, the expenses of preparing and producing the printed edition, distribution and advertising costs and royalty charges, the seller will also be affected by various other factors in determining the prices of printed music. One consideration is the potential market which determines the size, and, in turn, the costs of the initial print order. Another factor is competition in the particular area of music. For example, one piano methods course cannot be priced considerably out of line with others.

Many publishers use a formula of about six times the print costs to arrive at retail list prices, and three times print costs for wholesale prices.

These are usually one-half of the retail selling price. Thus, a printing cost of 25 cents for folios would lead to a $1.50 retail price.

A further factor in pricing printed music is whether the edition is part of a series in the serious music and educational fields. The cost of preparing a later issue may be reduced by the series' uniformity of style. Also, the advertising and promotion costs may be lessened by prior exploitation efforts. In addition, there may be an assurance of sales of a later issue. Prior purchasers, such as guitar teachers buying a methods series, are likely to be interested in acquiring later editions in the series.

A folio bearing the name and picture of a popular recording artist, as for example a folio of The Beatles' hits, has increased sales potential as a consequence of the endorsement. The attraction of the endorsement may enable the publisher to fix prices which are higher than usual. Frequently, large sums are paid to the endorsing artist either as a flat sum or as an advance against royalties. These often equal the 10 per cent of wholesale price paid to composers.

Finally, reprints of printed music may justify lower prices. The initial costs of preparation have been recouped, and lower prices may still ensure satisfactory profits. Reprints are of special importance in sales to educational institutions which may continue to reorder once the edition is a part of the curriculum.

FOREIGN SALES

Usually, popular printed music is not exported. Instead, it is licensed for printing and sales to foreign licensees or agents. These are generally referred to as subpublishers. Under the terms of the license, the foreign subpublisher agrees to pay the American publisher a royalty which is commonly 10 per cent, but may increase up to about 12.5 per cent, of the foreign retail selling price. The receipts by the American publisher from the subpublisher are usually divided equally between the American writer and the American publisher.

If a foreign subpublisher administers the collection of mechanical license fees and performance fees, this, as a rule, will be more lucrative than the handling of printed editions. Some American publishers encourage printing in a foreign country. This is done by providing, in contracts with subpublishers, that the subpublisher's share of mechanical license fees and performance fees will be less for unprinted songs than for those that are printed. The question whether folio publication, as distinguished from sheet music, satisfies this printing provision should be covered in the agreement with the subpublisher.

Printing may be especially important in the case of motion picture songs originating in films scored by members of the British Performing Right Society. Under the rules of the Society, unless the music has been commercially recorded, the publisher who fails to print will not participate in motion picture performance fees collected from theatres outside the United States. In that case, the writer will receive the so-called publisher's share as well as the writer's share of fees.

MAILING PRIVILEGES

The music publishing, as well as the phonograph record, industry is the beneficiary of a favorable postage policy of the United States government. Special fourth class rates are applicable to the basic materials produced by the enterprises. Postage charges are 10 cents for the first pound and 5 cents for each additional pound or fraction thereof. The policy reason for this favored treatment is to encourage the widespread dissemination of educational and cultural materials, and thereby to foster a national cultural life.

Included in the fourth class rate category are printed music or music manuscripts, whether in bound or sheet music form. The rate applies regardless of the number of copies, provided that maximum size and weight of containers are observed. The rates are also applicable to sound recordings and, if in the same package, incidental announcements of sound recordings appearing on labels, sleeves, cartons or wrappers, or as loose enclosures, as well as scripts and guides for use with the recording.

The size of the package is limited to a length and girth combined of 100 inches. The weight of the package is restricted to 70 pounds.

Although many companies still use the outdated phrase "Educational Materials," the proper notation should be SPECIAL FOURTH CLASS RATE followed by PRINTED MUSIC or SOUND RECORDINGS or MANUSCRIPT, depending on the contents.

Enclosures with mailings of printed editions of music or music manuscripts are limited to invoices. There cannot be enclosed announcements of publication, reply envelopes, or cards.

6

BACKGROUND MUSIC AND TRANSCRIPTIONS

THE growing field of background music is to be distinguished from foreground music. The latter has goals of "show-stoppers" and million record hit singles which, in the words of Muzak executive Don O'Neill, attempt to "catch your ear and start you whistling." Background music, on the other hand, avoids being the center of attention. Whether it serves as background to dinner table conversation at a restaurant or as underscoring to a feature motion picture, it is a mood-setting accompaniment.

The music industry recognizes a division of the general field of background music into two parts. One part, sometimes referred to herein as "background music services," is generally identified with Muzak and its competitors. The other part is the background music, sometimes referred to herein as "film music," used in sound tracks for motion picture and television films. There is also the additional minor area of transcribed music for radio broadcasting.

Muzak describes its programming as ". . . functional music with a mission of relieving fatigue or boredom, dampening machine clatter, or simply relaxing people."

The field of background music for films was described by Judge John E. McGeehan, formerly a Justice of the Supreme Court of the State of New York. He was appointed under the 1960 ASCAP consent decree to examine periodically the design and conduct of the ASCAP survey of performances. In his 1963 report on ASCAP he stated:

> ". . . with the voracious consumption of background music by television, more people have heard music composed by any one of the

many active background composers within a very short period than have listened to the symphonic works of any one of the great composers in the whole history of the latter works. It is also true, however, that the works of the great symphonic composers have been listened to, whereas background music, however important it may be to the dramatic action, is heard and in most instances the hearers are not consciously aware of the music itself."

Both major areas of background music require special consideration in both business and legal aspects. Accordingly, the discussion in this chapter will, for the most part, deal separately with each type of background music.

BACKGROUND MUSIC SERVICES

Background music services are increasingly found in locations such as hotels, restaurants, bars, grills, taverns, factories, offices, banking institutions, stores, professional offices, ships, trains and airplanes. As in the case of Muzak, the music may be transmitted to locations by means of central studio facilities using FM multiplex broadcasting or leased telephone wires. Another method is the use of on-location equipment such as the tape playback apparatus sold by Minnesota Mining and Manufacturing ("3M"). In addition to Muzak and 3M, there are a number of other companies in the field, including Canteen Corporation and Seeburg.

Each of these background music services offer what is described in the applicable BMI public performance license as ". . . unobtrusive accompaniment to work, shopping, conversation, dining and relaxation."

The special problems relating to public performance and mechanical reproduction licenses for background music services are discussed hereinafter. Each will be better understood after a review of business practices in the field.

MUZAK

As indicative of various aspects of background music services, the organization and operations of Muzak will now be considered. Since its organization in 1934, Muzak has been an acknowledged leader in the field of background music services. Formerly an independent company, it has been a separate division of the Wrather Corporation since 1957.

The central offices of Muzak are in New York City. From these offices, the following activities are supervised.

PROGRAMMING: Muzak maintains a library of tens of thousands of individual selections, indexed on automated punchcards for programming needs. It adds as many as 30 new selections monthly.

LICENSING COPYRIGHTED WORKS: Muzak central offices, in consultation with their franchisees, negotiate public performance licenses with ASCAP and BMI, and allocate these licenses to franchised dealers who make license fee payments to ASCAP and BMI. The central offices also obtain reproduction licenses from music publishers for each song used, and pay the license fees centrally. A limited number of copyrights are owned by Muzak.

ARRANGING OF MUSIC: Muzak central offices engage free-lance arrangers and conductors.

RECORDING ACTIVITIES: All Muzak records are made in United States studios by members of the American Federation of Musicians. Each session is recorded in both stereo and monaural forms, but tapes are issued, in almost all cases, only in monaural form.

MANUFACTURING AND SHIPPING OF TAPES: Eight-hour tapes are centrally manufactured and then shipped under strict control to franchise holders, to be shipped after use to a further designated franchise holder.

EQUIPMENT APPROVAL: All subscribers must use approved audio equipment.

FRANCHISE ISSUANCE: Franchises are issued to the nearly 300 franchise holders throughout the world.

ADVERTISING AND PROMOTION: Muzak central offices handle the general advertising and promotion programs. These are aimed at subscribing locations rather than at individual listeners. The central offices also conduct a number of psychologically-oriented personnel and management studies geared to show industrial and office efficiency and savings through the use of background music.

The local activities of Muzak are handled through franchised dealers. Franchises are issued on a 10-year basis, and the local dealers perform the following functions:

SALES: Three to five year subscriptions are sold in four different categories: Industrial Programs, Office Programs, Public Area Programs (restaurants, hotels, etc.), and the relatively new and less important Travel Program (planes, ships, trains, etc.). Prices go up to four figures for monthly rates to some major accounts, in addition to initial basic charges for labor and equipment needed for installation.

SERVICE: Franchise holders send Muzak music to subscribers either by leased telephone lines or through special FM multiplex broadcast facilities. The tapes themselves are run through centrally located automated transmitters, specially cued to change programs as well as to deliver regular intervals of silence which are part of the industrial and office programs. Equipment maintenance is also a franchisee duty.

LICENSE FEE PAYMENTS: Each franchise holder separately accounts and pays to ASCAP and BMI.

Muzak lays great stress upon its particular qualities to distinguish its service from that of the restaurant proprietor who merely plays regular LP's. It claims to have "scientifically programmed background music arranged ingeniously to be unobtrusive and to render a subtle, subliminal impetus to efficiency and an environmental well-being." Its management studies are alleged to show the achievement of better personnel relationships in difficult situations involving machine clatter and office routine monotony. It claims that the background music encourages better attendance records. In accomplishing these results it is alleged that a certain uniformity of style of performance and arrangement is required in conjunction with identifiable melodies.

There may be contrasted with the central broadcasting services of Muzak, other companies' on-location equipment which is leased, loaned or sold to customers.

3M

Under the background music project of the 3M company, sales are made of a tape cartridge playback machine, and of tapes, each of which contains 700 compositions. The 3M equipment is alleged to be both cheaper to operate and maintain than other apparatus. It can be sold to users together with tapes, rather than leased with a maintenance contract for the equipment.

To date, all of the material in 3M tapes has been recorded in Europe so as to garner the advantages of lower recording costs for musicians, arrangers, copyists and studios. The recording activities of 3M require functions similar to those of Muzak. There are problems of programming, licensing of copyrighted works, arranging of music, hiring of musicians, and the manufacturing and shipping of tapes.

LICENSES FROM COPYRIGHT OWNERS

The licenses obtained by background music service companies such as Muzak and 3M from copyright proprietors for the mechanical reproduction of music by tape or other means are known as "transcription licenses." Correspondingly, the resultant tapes are frequently called "transcription tapes."

The terms of a transcription license issued by a copyright proprietor are subject to negotiation. Frequently, as in most licenses to Muzak, they are for a fixed term of years with a single payment covering all copies made of a composition during the term. Some licenses to Muzak run for three years and call for payment to a publisher of $12.50 for each selection appearing on the transcription.

An alternate license arrangement is $5 per year for each composition. The licenses may also provide that if the transcriptions are used for nationally sponsored broadcasts by radio or television stations, the licensee will pay 25 cents per station for each popular music composition and 50 cents for each show or film tune, or other composition.

Any use of a transcription beyond the original transcription license period requires an extension or renewal of the transcription license. Sometimes an option is acquired to extend the license beyond the initial period. This is obtained at the time of the original license, and is subject, in all instances, to an additional transcription license fee. The background music supplier, having made a substantial investment in arranging and producing the transcribed selection, may desire to extend the term of use beyond the initial term. The supplier's option to renew at a fixed price is good insurance that the product will be continually available.

A form of Muzak-type license used by the Harry Fox Office, which represents many publishers, is included as Appendix S. In the case of Muzak-type licensees, public performance licenses for the music are separately obtained from the performing rights organization (ASCAP or BMI). These licenses are discussed at page 66 hereinafter.

The form of license negotiated by the 3M company for its tape transcriptions, which are sold rather than leased to users, is substantially different from the traditional or Muzak form of transcription license. Instead of a fixed fee for a number of years regardless of the number of copies made, the 3M license calls for 5 cents a selection for each copy of a transcription tape that is sold. This represents 2 cents for a mechanical reproduction license, and 3 cents for a performance rights license. The 3-cent performance payment covers a three-year license period.

From the publishers' point of view, since 3M makes a final sale of its equipment to each location, a volume of sales is expected, and a royalty based on the number of copies sold has therefore been accepted by the publishers licensing to 3M.

The 3 cent-per-copy performing right fee under the 3M license is paid to BMI for the users' right to perform the BMI music on the 3M tapes. The same rate of compensation is applied in performance licenses received directly from publishers of ASCAP music on the 3M tapes. Pursuant to a Court consent decree entered into by ASCAP and the Antitrust Division of the Department of Justice, there is reserved to ASCAP publishers the non-exclusive right to grant performing right licenses. The licenses to 3M for ASCAP music have been negotiated pursuant to this reserved right.

The three-year performance right license begins on the date of sale of a 3M tape to each user. BMI or the licensor-publishers who are members of ASCAP will have the problem of policing the purchasers after the expiration of the three-year period. The 3M company has agreed to have each purchaser sign an agreement acknowledging the rights of the copyright proprietors. 3M will also notify purchasers before the end of the three-year period that their rights will expire, and that for continued use of the tape, an additional license from the copyright proprietors must be arranged. The names and addresses of the purchasers will be transmitted by the 3M company to the copyright proprietors.

COMPULSORY LICENSES AND TRANSCRIPTIONS

The question may arise as to why a mechanical reproduction for transcription purposes is different from "mechanical reproductions" for recording purposes to which the 2 cent compulsory license under Section 1(e) of the Copyright Act applies. In years past, the magic words "electrical transcription" seemed sufficient to show the difference from the "mechanical reproductions" entailed in cutting a disc. However, electronic processes are used in all tape recordings today and hardly a disc cut in today's market is not, at some stage of its processing, an electronic tape reproduction.

Various justifications have been advanced for excluding transcriptions from the compulsory license provisions. It may be contended that the framers of the compulsory license provision in 1909 intended to apply it only to phonograph records and player-piano rolls, bands and cylinders. These were the recording devices known and described at the legislative hearings, and the ones set forth in the statute. Therefore, it may be asserted, makers of transcriptions may not invoke compulsory licenses.

Furthermore, under the Copyright Act, a person filing a compulsory license must make "similar use" of the copyrighted work, as compared to the use previously made or authorized by the copyright proprietor. It may be argued that the use is dissimilar since a conventional recording, which may be the only prior use sanctioned by the copyright owner, is made primarily for sale to the home market. Transcriptions are intended for public performances over the air or in public places.

On the other hand, it may be asserted that the use is similar since records for the home market are almost invariably dispatched to disc jockeys and stations to obtain public exposure through broadcast performances. Or, even more directly, for proof of similar use, reference may be made to Muzak-type licenses already in existence as to a composition.

Another contention by opponents of the applicability of compulsory licenses is that transcriptions are characterized by special arrangements. In fact, the background music suppliers of transcriptions claim that their arrangements are their trademarks. These arrangements induce a mood of inattention which is anathema to most records manufactured for sale to the public. It is asserted that these arrangements also remove transcriptions from the "similar use" category. In any event, goes the argument, the copyright owner is entitled to require a special license under his exclusive right, under the Copyright Act, "to arrange and adapt" the musical work. In reply, it may be contended that the right of mechanical reproduction under compulsory licensing implies some latitude and flexibility with respect to preparing instrumental or vocal arrangements, and this latitude is now observed in the field of conventional recordings.

Regardless of the technical arguments as to why compulsory licenses may or may not apply, a practical answer is that customs and usages in the industry recognize that a transcription license should be sought. However, the technical arguments in favor of compulsory licenses undoubtedly tend to keep in check the fees requested by publishers for transcription licenses.

COPYRIGHT REVISION BILLS

The ambiguities noted above in respect to the application of compulsory licenses have been recognized by the draftsmen of the now pending Copyright Revision Bills. Section 113(a)(1) of H.R. 4347 S. 1006 (89th Cong. 2nd Session) reads:

"A person may obtain a compulsory license only if his primary purpose in making phonorecords is to distribute them to the public for private use."

Transcriptions are not distributed to the public at large in most instances but rather to a limited group of commercial users.

The bills in Section 113(a)(2) would clarify the "similar use" requirement for a compulsory license now contained in the Copyright Act. This is done by including in compulsory licenses the "privilege of making a musical arrangement of the work to the extent necessary to conform it to the style or manner of interpretation of the performance involved, but the arrangement shall not change the basic melody or fundamental character of the work. . . ."

PUBLIC PERFORMANCE LICENSES

Background music services to offices, factories and public places entail public performances of the music. These are deemed to be for profit, under the standards of the Copyright Act, and must be licensed by the copyright proprietors of the music or their agents. Licenses for such performances can be obtained from ASCAP, BMI and SESAC.

As noted previously, 3M, in respect to ASCAP music, has acquired direct licenses from the copyright proprietors, although it has negotiated a license from BMI for the BMI music contained in its tapes.

Forms of ASCAP and BMI background music service license agreements are included as Appendixes T and U respectively. These licenses are issued to the supplier of the services and not to the ultimate user, such as a factory or restaurant. ASCAP's fees are in substance 3½ per cent of the gross receipts charged by the background music supplier to most premises other than those establishments serving food and beverages and those selling or offering goods or services to the public. For the excepted premises the fee is usually $27 per establishment for a year. The fees of BMI are in essence ½ per cent of the gross receipts charged by the background music supplier to industrial premises, and 1 per cent of such gross receipts in the case of other users. BMI licenses specifically provide in certain instances for annual minimum charges for each location. The licenses should be read to ascertain the charges for a particular type of business. For example, BMI's minimum charge is $5 for each hotel and each night club.

SESAC generally licenses background music services on a fixed fee basis for each outlet, regardless of the type of business or the gross receipts involved.

PERFORMING RIGHT ORGANIZATION DISTRIBUTIONS

ASCAP distributions to publishers and writers of collections for background music in stores, factories, etc. are aided by the submission to ASCAP of music cue sheets prepared by the background music supplier. These show the actual compositions used and the time involved in the performance. ASCAP makes special distribution of the funds received from this category of users. It accounts to its writer and publisher members on separate "wired music" distribution reports. These list the compositions involved and the amounts earned. BMI and most SESAC payments for this category are not segregated. Such funds received by BMI and SESAC have been distributed as a part of their regular performance fee distribution. However, as to 3M payments, BMI expects to make a special distribution. As to 3M, SESAC charges a combined fee for performance and transcription licenses and distributes the moneys to affiliates as if received for mechanical licenses.

FILM MUSIC

As noted previously, a significant and separate area of background music is that used as accompaniment to motion picture and television films. An ASCAP definition of background music follows:

"Background music shall mean mood, atmosphere, or thematic music performed as background to some non-musical subject matter. . . . A vocal or a visual instrumental rendition which is a principal focus of audience attention shall not be regarded as background music regardless of the context in which performed."

Background music may be specifically composed, arranged and performed, as is prevalent in feature motion pictures produced in the United States. It may also consist of specially edited sound tracks originating in sound track libraries. This is frequently the case in industrial films, and sometimes occurs in television films.

Music used in sound tracks requires copyright synchronization licenses from music publishers or other copyright proprietors, as well as public performance licenses.

SYNCHRONIZATION LICENSES

When background music is recorded on the sound track of a theatrical or television film, the form of license from a copyright owner is called a "synchronization" license. Synchronization is a word which does not appear in the Copyright Act, but it is recognized as covering the act of mechanical reproduction of music in a synchronized relationship to the dramatic action of the film.

Synchronization licenses, as well as transcription licenses, are most often handled through the Office of Harry Fox, Trustee, on behalf of the many publishers associated with that office. Some publishers issue such licenses either directly or through other agents. A copy of a publisher-television synchronization license is included as Appendix V. SESAC publishers issue both transcription and synchronization licenses through SESAC.

Background music synchronization licenses will usually be for a fixed fee. They will frequently specify the number and lengths of playings that the producer may utilize, the type of production authorized, the geographic area of such use, and a limited term of years during which the license will be effective.

In recent years, the rate of license fees for television has dropped substantially, to as low as $25 to $50 per use. This is due to several factors. The publishers take into consideration the additional ASCAP or BMI performance credits granted when the film is shown on television. There is also competition from other publishers and from sound track libraries. A copy of a sound track library synchronization license is included as Appendix W.

Only a relatively small amount of background music stems from publisher licenses, since original background music composers and, to a lesser extent, sound track libraries, supply the bulk. Another source of music available for additional background music synchronization is music in earlier films. This is due to the free synchronization right which had been reserved by many producers on original music composed for their films.

PERFORMING RIGHT LICENSES

Television film producers do not request a performance license for the music in their films; the broadcasting stations are licensed by the performing right organizations. Theatrical film producers need not necessarily obtain a performance license for exhibitions outside the United States, since the theatres and broadcasters in foreign countries are licensed by the local performing right organizations. However, the producers will ordinarily acquire a performance license for United States theatrical performance.

This is because ASCAP, by a court decree, is prohibited from requiring licenses from theatres for ASCAP music in films. The performance license will be granted by original music composers when they assign synchronization rights. Publishers, either directly or through the Harry Fox Office, license United States performance rights at the same time as synchronization rights.

Television stations in the United States are licensed in almost all cases under blanket licenses issued by ASCAP, BMI and SESAC. Under licenses issued by ASCAP and BMI, the fees charged the stations are a percentage of their gross receipts. SESAC's fees are based on fixed amounts; these vary in accordance with such factors as location, hours and power of the station.

In rare instances, a television station in the United States may obtain a "per program" license from ASCAP. In its "per program" license, ASCAP charges a lesser rate for films, originally produced for theatres, without feature music than for similar films which include vocals or other feature music.

ASCAP AND BMI DISTRIBUTIONS FOR BACKGROUND MUSIC

There has been much controversy over the question of the relative weight of film background music as against film feature music. The standard generally applied by ASCAP and BMI is that payment on a pure durational basis would not fairly reflect the worth of each performance. They give greater weight to feature music in determining distributions of performance fees.

In general, BMI makes no distinction, for payment purposes, among equal segments of background music; all portions of the music are treated equally.

Under the ASCAP distribution format well-established works with a specified minimum of past feature performances are deemed "qualifying" works. When these works are used for background music, they earn considerably more under the ASCAP distribution rules than other background music works which are not so qualified. In recent years ASCAP has followed Judge McGeehan's recommendations that it lessen the credit difference between qualifying and non-qualifying works used for similar purposes. Thus, the latest change was to increase from 20 per cent to 25 per cent of a feature performance credit the value of the performance of three minutes of non-qualifying background music.

Separate and apart from the actual rates of payment applied, there are various other distinctions in the payment formulas of ASCAP and BMI for background music. BMI lowers the payment rate by one-third for non-prime time versus prime time (6:00-11:00 P.M.) showings on television, whereas ASCAP does not so distinguish. BMI reduces the payment rate progressively as to the minutes of music in excess of 50 per cent of a television show, except for feature films previously appearing in American theatres. ASCAP's rates, based on duration, for background music are not reduced regardless of the extent of the background music in a program, although there are special maximum credit provisions applying to the repetition of themes, qualifying works, and to a limited number of other printed or recorded works.

For background music in network television or radio programs appearing four or more times a week, ASCAP curtails credits to 25 per cent of the otherwise applicable credit. This particularly limits the accumulation of credits for background music in soap operas and other programs which are frequently shown. BMI diminishes credits by 50 per cent for any daytime series program on network television four or more times a week.

The payment distribution formulas of ASCAP and BMI are constantly subject to change and reference should be made to those organizations for the rules applicable at any given time.

COMPOSERS OF TELEVISION MUSIC

The applicable guild of background music composers is the Composers and Lyricists Guild of America (CLGA). This guild does not require that any film, whether theatrical or television, contain original music. It sets standards and general terms and conditions of employment to the extent that the producer chooses to employ original music composers.

In 1962, the Columbia Broadcasting System reported that payments to original music composers were running at a rate of $50.00 to $60.00 per minute of original music on its shows. The 1965 CLGA agreement provides for minimum weekly salary standards for composers, and there is no stipulated sum per minute of music.

The agreement sets forth minimum writer royalty payments if the original music is assigned for publication. A copy of the writer minimum compensation and royalty provisions in the CLGA agreement is included as Appendix X. The composer remains entitled to collect the writer's share of performance right payments through his affiliated performing rights organization.

The CLGA agreement is adhered to by most important television producers.

SOUND TRACK LIBRARIES

When not utilizing live musicians for underscoring, producers resort to various sound track libraries. Some of these are: Capitol Records, Inc., Boosey & Hawkes, Inc. and Francis Day & Hunter Inc. Libraries license directly and not through an agent such as the Harry Fox Office. A library is a categorized, alphabetized collection of recordings available to fit background music needs. Thus one may request music suitable for Autumn or a Zebra. A library usually adheres to published rate cards with rates depending on the type of film (e.g., industrial show or commercial television) and the number and duration of usages. A copy of a rate card is included as Appendix Y.

Heavy usage of sound track libraries occurs in travelogues and industrial film productions. In these instances, the combination of a restricted budget with limited sound requirements permits less reliance on original music.

A common sound track library rate system is based on the "needle drop" method of computing payments for recordings on tape or on discs used by television producers on a non-exclusive basis. Under this method, it is usual for a one-time fixed payment (e.g., $20.00) to be made by the user for each continuous portion of the recording employed. An incentive to the licensor for this form of arrangement is his reservation of the right to collect ASCAP or BMI performance fees.

UNION STANDARDS

Sound track libraries for film purposes are almost wholly derived from foreign recordings. The American Federation of Musicians has repeatedly appealed without success to Congress to ban the importation of foreign music tapes and tracks.

The use of sound track libraries for feature and television films, however, has been limited significantly by musician union agreements applicable to pictures produced in the United States and Canada. Signatories to agreements with the union have contracted that all such films must be scored in the United States and Canada. No sound track library music may appear in the theatrical films. Television films are required to employ music recorded live by union musicians except that, in respect of a television series, music recorded for any picture in the series may be reused to score other pictures in the series produced for the same broadcasting season. But there are union requirements as to the minimum amount of fresh union-scored music for a given series. For example, for 13 one-half hour dramatic pictures there must be a total of 21 scoring hours.

The union agreement permits library music or "historical" music sound tracks to be combined with new union made music in documentaries if the minimum live scoring standards for other films are complied with and if the scoring is done by an orchestra of a minimum size. There is no requirement as to the size of an orchestra which scores the music for other films.

RADIO BROADCAST TRANSCRIPTIONS

In years past, there were firms which provided a significant source of program material in transcription form. A ready-made half-hour transcribed radio program would extend some of the advantages of network-style programming to unaffiliated stations. The typical license for music used on such shows would be at a rate of 25 cents per song for each station broadcasting the transcription if the song were a popular one, and double that amount if the song originated in a show or film. Accordingly, a payment of $37.50 for a 150-station usage of a song would be expected.

In today's radio broadcasting, transcriptions are used for special programming introductions, for themes, background music and for sports breaks. They are rarely employed for full programs except for public service programs such as those presented by the Veterans Administration, Treasury Department and Armed Forces. These transcriptions are distributed free of charge to stations.

At present, there is a greater interest in transcriptions on the part of broadcasters since the Federal Communications Commission ruled that FM broadcasters cannot duplicate more than 50 per cent of the programs of AM stations in the same area in population centers of more than 100,000.

It is now common for publishers to license such transcription use through the Harry Fox Office at a rate per song of $5.00 a year or $12.50

for 3 years, as in the case of the Muzak-type licenses. While the 25 cents and 50 cents per song fee is still available, the Fox Office has found that policing the fee is unduly burdensome and, therefore, the fixed fee license is preferred.

An agreement in use by a modern transcription company provides for a two-year lease to the broadcast user of the transcription library. The lease grants exclusive rights for the local broadcast area, at monthly rental rates varying with the size and location of the station. The transcription library consists of tapes and discs covering sound effects, time and weather announcements, tailored introductions of the local station's programs, and backgrounds for commercials and public service announcements. The music used on the transcriptions is subject to ASCAP or BMI licenses.

7

TAPE CARTRIDGES

THE tape cartridge development has ignited the imagination of both
the automotive and the music-record industries. Its market is still minute
when compared to the size of the record business, but its burgeoning
growth has impressed most observers.

In a relatively short period of time, the automotive field has seen the
cartridge playback emerge as one of its strongest selling accessories. With
the sale of players and car installations has come an increasing traffic in
recorded cartridges.

The music-record industry sees great potential in this development.
The cartridge promises to open a vast new market for recordings, and with
it, a heretofore untapped source of additional revenue for record companies, artists, music publishers, composers and writers. The cartridge
device is expected to broaden considerably the base of the industry by
exposing recorded product in sales sectors previously unknown to discs.
In addition to record stores, tape cartridges today are being sold by car
dealers, automotive accessory houses, and even in filling stations, among
other retail outlets.

Its sales volume, of course, will be significantly increased after the
cartridge crosses the threshold from the garage into the home. This appears inevitable as a growing number of home equipment manufacturers
are featuring cartridge playback units in their new models. These range
from purse-sized portables to cartridge players in console combinations.

Early in 1966, George R. Marek, vice president and general manager of the RCA Victor Record Division, predicted that cartridge sales would approximate the phonograph record dollar volume within five years.

CARTRIDGE HISTORY

The tape cartridge concept of reproducing recorded music was born during the mid-fifties. It simplifies the use of tape by eliminating the threading required by a conventional reel-to-reel tape recorder.

This is accomplished by the manufacturer encasing the tape in a container or cartridge. To hear the recording, one merely inserts the cartridge into a specially designed playback.

There are various types of tape cartridges. The first significant system was introduced by RCA Victor in 1958. This consists of a reel-to-reel assembly sealed in a plastic container. Its operation is quite similar to that of a regular reel-to-reel arrangement with the exception, of course, that both reels are enclosed in a cartridge.

This twin-spool cartridge approach, with various significant refinements, is still followed today, but its use is far greater overseas than in this country. Of the several applications of the reel-to-reel cartridge concept, the Philips cassette enjoys the greatest following abroad.

CONTINUOUS LOOP PRINCIPLE

In the United States, the method most widely employed in the so-called automobile tape cartridge system utilizes a single spool, with a continuous loop tape which automatically rewinds itself as it plays. This is achieved by splicing together both ends of the tape to form the continuous or "endless" loop. The cartridge is designed to allow the tape to "feed" or unwind from the center of the spool, pass across the tape playback head at 3¾ i.p.s., and then rewind itself around the circumference of the same spool.

This is the basic operating principle in almost all tape cartridges used in American cars. Different applications of this principle, however, have created several keenly competitive, incompatible cartridge systems.

FIDELIPAC

Of these systems, the one which has been in use the longest is the

Fidelipac. It was invented by George Eash, and is now owned and manufactured by TelePro Industries, Inc. of Cherry Hill, New Jersey. For a number of years, this cartridge was used primarily by radio station transcription services for recorded jingles, theme music, sound effects, time and weather announcements, and other material. The continuous loop cartridge is still used extensively by the broadcasting industry.

Earl Muntz is generally credited with being the first to market the tape cartridge for automotive use. In 1962, prior to his present association with Muntz Stereo-Pak, Inc., he helped to form a firm in Los Angeles, California, known as Muntz Music, Inc., later called Autostereo, Inc., which installed tape cartridge playbacks in automobiles. This equipment played 4-track stereophonic tape encased in the Fidelipac cartridge.

Muntz acquired the rights to several record company catalogs. He duplicated their albums in cartridge form so that he could sell music to his playback equipment customers. Autostereo and the other firms which soon followed it into the car tape field apparently enjoyed a brisk business.

At this point, the 4-track Fidelipac cartridge was generally considered to be the standard of the fledgling automobile tape industry. Its sales, however, were centered mainly in California, Texas and Florida. While there were buyers in other sections of the country, they were comparatively few.

LEAR JET

In the spring of 1965, the car tape field took on a national prominence. William Lear, Sr., president of the Lear Jet Corp., disclosed that his firm had developed a different type of continuous loop cartridge and playback system, and that it would launch it in conjunction with RCA Victor and the Ford Motor Co. RCA Victor said it would make its recordings available exclusively in this "Stereo-8" system. The Ford Motor Co. announced that it would factory-install equipment to play the new cartridge in its 1966 car models.

While the Lear cartridge follows the same basic continuous loop principle mentioned above, it has two major changes which keep it from being used in a Fidelipac-type playback, and, thus, make the two systems incompatible. In addition to a different method whereby the tape is propelled within the cartridge, the new system plays 8-track tape as opposed to Fidelipac's 4-track. Both operate at 3¾ i.p.s.

The Ford Motor Co. launched an intensive national advertising campaign on behalf of the new "Stereo-8" cartridge system, using television, mass circulation consumer magazines and daily newspapers. This resulted in consumers becoming aware of the automobile tape cartridge concept on a nationwide scale, thus spreading the market beyond the few isolated areas where it had previously existed.

Ford's initial sales success with Stereo-8 prompted the two other major automobile manufacturers, Chrysler and General Motors, to embrace the same 8-track system. The promise of a considerably expanded market for tape in automobiles spurred the other major record companies to enter the field. Capitol, Columbia and Decca announced that they would duplicate their albums in Lear-type 8-track form. In addition, Decca said it would issue its releases in Fidelipac-type 4-track as well.

ORRTRONICS

Shortly after Lear unveiled his Stereo-8, still another continuous loop system was introduced, the Orrtronics cartridge. This is similar to the Lear in that it uses 8-track 3¾ i.p.s. stereophonic tape. However, this system calls for the tape to travel across the tape head on a horizontal plane as opposed to the vertical system employed in the other two cartridges. As a result, the Orrtronics cartridge is incompatible with the equipment playing the other two systems. A comparatively small number of these cartridges have been sold, and, therefore, this system appears to be a relatively insignificant factor in the battle of the cartridge system.

RECORD COMPANIES

Today, almost all the important record companies are represented by some albums in cartridge form. Some of the labels have product available in all three cartridge systems. From the standpoint of quantity, more labels are represented in the two major systems, the Fidelipac-type 4-track and the Lear-type 8-track. The Big Three record companies — Capitol, Columbia and RCA Victor — are sticking exclusively to the Lear-type cartridge.

These firms, along with Decca and several other companies, have announced that they will handle their own tape cartridge duplication and marketing. Most of the labels, however, assign cartridge rights to firms who duplicate and market the product as in the conventional reel-to-reel tape field.

COMPATIBLE PLAYBACKS

The incompatibility problem may be eased somewhat by the development of a playback designed to operate with both the Fidelipac-type 4-track and the Lear-type 8-track cartridge. Several equipment manufacturers have introduced the combined 4- and 8-track players.

CARTRIDGE SUPPLIERS

Cartridges are supplied by several manufacturers. The Lear Jet Corp. manufactures and sells its Stereo-8 cartridge. Similarly, TelePro Industries, Inc. manufactures and furnishes its Fidelipac 4-track container. However, several manufacturers have announced that they will make cartridges which will fit machines which play the Stereo-8 cartridge. TelePro has concluded an arrangement with Capitol Records to supply the label with 8-track cartridges compatible with the Lear Stereo-8 used by RCA Victor. In addition, TelePro has licensed Capitol to manufacture its own 8-track cartridges should the record company choose to produce its own containers.

The Amerline Corp. of Chicago, Illinois, and Audio Devices, Inc. of New York, New York, have also announced that they will manufacture 8-track cartridges compatible with the Stereo-8.

MECHANICAL REPRODUCTION LICENSES

With respect to cartridges, mechanical reproduction licenses must be obtained from the copyright owners of the music contained in the cartridge. Cartridges for home or auto use are treated the same as phonograph discs with regard to license rates. The statutory compulsory license rate of 2 cents per composition is applied as the maximum license rate in licenses issued by music publishers or through the Harry Fox Office. Ordinarily, this amount will be payable for each cartridge manufactured and sold. It is the position of the Harry Fox Office that the statutory rate of 2 cents per tune will prevail, regardless of any lower rate which may have been negotiated for the use of that tune in the original disc version.

In the event a tape cartridge is used in commercial background music systems, the Harry Fox Office requires a transcription license at a negotiated rate. Reference should be made to Chapter 6 entitled "Background Music and Transcriptions" for a discussion of these licenses.

PERFORMANCE LICENSES

The Copyright Act grants exclusive rights to the copyright owner in respect of public performances for profit. The performance of a cartridge in an automobile or at home is for private and not public use. In addition, such performances are not for profit. The treatment is parallel to that of phonograph discs, in that a performance license is not sought or required.

LICENSING OF CARTRIDGE RIGHTS

For years record companies have licensed to Ampex and similar companies the right to manufacture and sell reel-to-reel tape versions of their recordings. The royalty to the licensor has varied. The level of royalties has tended to increase because of the intense competition among companies manufacturing tapes. Royalties of approximately 10 to 12½ per cent of the suggested retail list price (less any excise tax and an allowance for packaging) of 90 to 100 per cent of records sold are common. Royalty rates are likely to increase in proportion to the desirability of a particular record catalog. They may decrease should the record company require that a greater number of different releases be issued. Attractive money advances or guarantees may also effect a lower royalty. Licensing ordinarily is for a period of years, usually for a three year term. Grants of exclusive reel-to-reel rights have been common, although some tape manufacturers have accepted non-exclusive rights.

Cartridge licensing provisions will approximate the terms of reel-to-reel licensing, with certain differences. Non-exclusive rights are more prevalent in the cartridge field; the same cartridges embodying the same recording may be marketed by several different companies. The severe competition for cartridge rights and the experimental stage of cartridge marketing have encouraged a decrease in the period of rights to as little as a year and even less. The cartridges' greater market potential, compared to reel-to-reel, prompts duplicators to offer larger money advances or guarantees for the cartridge rights than in reel-to-reel licensing.

ROYALTY OBLIGATIONS

Under both reel-to-reel and cartridge licensing, the tape company pays royalties to the licensing record company, is obligated to pay mechanical license fees to the copyright proprietors and makes payments based on sales to the Recording Industries Music Performance Trust Funds. The latter were established pursuant to agreements between the record companies and the American Federation of Musicians.

A subject of negotiations between a tape company and a record company is whether these fees will be paid initially to the record company which will pass them on to the copyright owners and the Trust Funds, or whether the payments will be made directly to the ultimate recipients. Under the Trust Funds agreements, the record company is prohibited from licensing its master recordings to a tape company in the United States or Canada unless that company is or becomes a party to agreements with the Trust Funds administrators.

If the tape company is a party to such agreements, the record company is not responsible to the Funds for payments due on the sale of tape cartridges. The record company may be satisfied with and even prefer direct payments to the Funds by an established and reputable tape company. Should the record company insist on being an intermediary so as to police payments to the Funds, the record company's obligation to pay the Funds would be limited to the moneys received from the tape company for transmission to the Funds.

The company which duplicates and markets tapes appears to be a "manufacturer" under Section 1(e) of the Copyright Act. Therefore, it is responsible for mechanical reproduction fees to the copyright owners of the music contained in the tape cartridges. According to the statute, the fees are "to be paid by the manufacturer thereof." Ordinarily the record company is willing to rely on the contractual obligation of the tape company to make payments to the copyright owners. However, the record company may fear possible claims that it has remained a principal in the tape distribution. In that event, it may require payment of copyright fees through the record company.

MINIMUM ROYALTY BASE

Chaotic and varying retail list prices suggested by different competing tape cartridge manufacturers may distress a licensing record company. If royalties are based solely on suggested retail prices, the record company can not forecast the royalties it will collect on each unit sold. Complications also result from the practice of combining more than one LP in a single cartridge. These may be sold at prices that approximate that of only one LP. For appropriate protection, the record company can stipulate that its royalty shall be no less than a given figure for each LP represented in a sold cartridge.

TAXES AND PACKAGING

In computing the retail list price upon which royalties will be based, it is customary to deduct any excise taxes and an allowance for packaging. Although in some instances the packaging deduction will be limited to the cost of empty cartridges, in others the deductions will also include allocations for other elements such as art work.

OTHER CONTRACTUAL STIPULATIONS

A provision which appears sometimes in both reel-to-reel and cartridge licensing agreements grants the record company the right to purchase completed product from the tape company at a substantial discount below the suggested retail list price. Thereby, if the grant of rights to the tape company is non-exclusive, the record company bolsters its right to enter the tape distribution market at any time in competition with the tape company. In effect, the record company will have arranged for its tape duplication on a custom basis.

From the prior discussion of reel-to-reel tape and cartridge licensing agreements, it is apparent that certain elements therein exist in agreements for licensing masters to foreign record companies. The latter contracts have been considered in detail in Chapter 2 entitled "Foreign Record Deals," in *This Business of Music,** and reference should be made to that chapter for the discussion therein.

Among additional elements in foreign licensing contracts, which should be weighed in the licensing of tape and cartridge rights are: (1) quality controls imposed by the record company, (2) issuance of the tapes and cartridges on the record company's label, (3) the record company's reservation of the right to license record clubs to manufacture tapes and cartridges, (4) whether the licensor's recordings may be coupled by the tape company with each other or with those of other licensors, (5) methods for servicing the tape company with samples of the licensor's records and other materials, (6) handling of tapes and other materials on termination of the license, (7) accounting and auditing rights, (8) appropriate default clauses, and (9) the right to arbitration in the event of disputes.

There is included as Appendix Z a typical form of agreement between a tape company and a record company with respect to cartridge rights.

---

* Sidney Shemel and M. William Krasilovsky (New York, 1964) p. 18ff.

UNAUTHORIZED DUBBING

Some dealers have embarked on a program of making tapes or tape cartridges to order for customers by duplicating discs. The justification offered for this practice is that tapes or tape cartridges of certain recordings are not available, and the customer is being rendered a service. For example, a customer may state that he is interested in a tape of the latest LP of Ferrante and Teicher. Assuming that a tape has not been made available by the record manufacturer, the dealer would then play the LP on duplicating equipment which produces a tape or cartridge to order.

Clearly, in such circumstances, the manufacturer is losing the profit he is entitled to derive from the sale of his product, the artist is deprived of royalties, the music copyright owner fails to receive mechanical royalties and the Recording Industries Music Performance Trust Funds will not be paid its due royalties.

The dealer may believe that he is acting within the law. This belief appears to be unfounded. A suit has been commenced by music publishers against such a dealer. A basis for the suit is the contention that the Copyright Act has been violated through the unlawful making and sale of copies of copyrighted music without the permission of the copyright owners.

Among the exclusive rights granted to copyright proprietors by the Copyright Act are rights under Section 1 to "copy, and vend," "to make or procure the making of any . . . record thereof," and "to . . . produce, or reproduce it in any manner or by any method whatsoever." No application for a license has been made by the dealer to the copyright owner or his agent, nor has there been any attempt to rely on the compulsory licensing provisions of Sections 1(e) and 101(e) of the Copyright Act. Even if a compulsory license were sought, copyright owners, as in the case of transcriptions (see discussion at page 64), may take the position that compulsory license provisions are not applicable.

Furthermore the record manufacturer and the recording artist would appear to be able to invoke at least the legal doctrine of unfair competition in order to protect their rights through suits for injunctions and for damages.

Since there is usually no counterfeiting of labels involved in the unauthorized duplication, the practice would not fall foul of the Federal anticounterfeiting law passed in 1962 to permit the criminal prosecution of record counterfeiters.*

In principle, the foregoing legal problems applicable to dubbing by dealers are also technically relevant to dubbing in the home. This is not presently a widespread practice due to expense, time and inconvenience.

---

* In 1966 New York State passed a law forbidding unauthorized duplication of records for the purpose of sale or public performance for profit and making the violation a criminal misdemeanor.

PROPOSED COPYRIGHT PROTECTION

Pursuant to the pending bills before Congress for the proposed revision of the Copyright Act, sound recordings, which are defined so as to include tapes and cartridges, would be protected against unauthorized duplication under copyright principles. The bills provide that sound recordings shall be the subject of copyright, with rights limited to the exclusive right to reproduce and distribute copies.

For copyright protection of records, the surface of the recording or its label or container would have to include a copyright notice. This notice would consist of the symbol ®, the year of first publication of the record, and the name of the recording's copyright owner.

PART THREE

APPENDIX

Appendix A

EMPLOYMENT OUTLOOK FOR MUSICIANS, MUSIC TEACHERS,
SINGERS AND SINGING TEACHERS
(Extracts from 1963-1964 Report by U.S. Department
of Labor on Employment Outlook in the Performing Arts)

The performing arts include music, acting, and the dance. The interest in and attraction of careers in this field are so great that the number of first-rate artists seeking employment is generally much larger than the number of full-time employment opportunities available. As a result, many performers supplement their incomes by teaching, and others have to work much of the time in different types of occupations.

The difficulty of earning a living as a performer is one of the facts young people should bear in mind in considering an artistic career. They should, therefore, consider the possible advantages of making their art a hobby rather than a field of work. Aspiring young artists must usually spend many years in intensive training and practice before they are ready for public performances. A person needs not only great natural talent but also determination, a willingness to work long and hard, and an overwhelming interest in his chosen field — a love for it so great that, despite all obstacles he would rather work in it than in any other occupation.

The statements which follow this introduction give detailed information on the instrumental musician, singer, actor, and dancer as performing artists and in related work. Many men and women with an interest and talent in music are also employed as directors of church choirs or school choruses or as orchestra or band conductors. A few with great creative talent work chiefly as composers of music. Other musicians arrange or adapt melodies for orchestras or bands; still others (copyists) copy parts for individual instruments from the musical scores written by arrangers. Similarly, a few people with ballet training and originality work as choreographers, who design new ballets or other types of dance performances, and some are dance directors. Another small field of employment, to which people with executive ability and a knowledge of acting and of production problems can sometimes progress, is that of directing or producing stage, television, or motion picture productions.

MUSICIANS AND MUSIC TEACHERS

NATURE OF WORK

Professional musicians — whether they play the piano, violin, or trumpet in a symphony orchestra, dance band, or "jazz combo" — have behind them many years of study and intensive practice. Although most musicians play only one instrument, many are qualified to play two or more — for example, the saxophone and clarinet, oboe and English horn, or piano and organ. As a rule, musicians also specialize in either classical or popular music; only a few play both types professionally.

In a symphony orchestra, 85 to 100 or more musicians play together under the direction of a conductor. About half the musicians in the orchestra play the strings — violins, violas, cellos, and double basses. Smaller numbers play the brass — trombones, trumpets, French horns, and tubas; and the woodwinds — oboes, flutes, piccolos, clarinets, English horns, and bassoons; and a few play the drums, cymbals, and other percussion instruments. Usually the orchestra also has among its members a pianist and one or two harpists. Each orchestra player has attained great technical skill in playing his particular instrument, and they play together with great precision. The musicians in the "first chairs" — the leading players of each kind of instrument — are especially fine artists and can play any solos called for by the parts for their instruments.

Musicians trained in classical music also play in opera and theater orchestras and for other kinds of performances needing orchestral accompaniments. Some form small groups — a string quartet or a trio (made up of a violinist, a cellist, and a pianist, for example) — which give concerts of chamber music. Many pianists serve as accompanists for vocal or instrumental soloists or choral groups or provide background music in restaurants or other places. Most organists play in churches, often directing the choir as well as playing the organ. A very few exceptionally brilliant and well known musicians — chiefly pianists and violinists — become concert artists, giving their own concerts and appearing as soloists with symphony orchestras. Orchestras, chamber music groups, and individual artists often make recordings.

Musicians who specialize in popular music usually play the trumpet, trombone, clarinet, saxophone, or one of the "rhythm" instruments — the piano, string bass, drums, or guitar. Dance bands using these instruments play in nightclubs, restaurants, and at special parties. The best known bands and solo performers sometimes give concerts and perform on television. They also make recordings.

Many musicians, in addition to their work as performers, give private lessons in their own studios or in pupils' homes. More than half of the people primarily employed as instrumental musicians (estimated at about 100,000 in 1962) teach in the Nation's schools and colleges and are seldom, if ever, paid for performing. These teachers may be members of the faculty of music schools or conservatories or of colleges which offer instruction in instrumental music. Some are music teachers in elementary or secondary schools where they direct vocal and instrumental music programs, teach music appreciation, and may also give group instruction on an instrument.

In addition to the people primarily employed as musicians or music teachers, thousands of qualified instrumentalists have other full-time jobs and only occasionally are paid for work in the field of music. Most of these part-time musicians belong to dance bands which are hired to play at private parties or for other special occasions. Many of those with a background in classical music play occasionally in an orchestra or for other performances, or do some part-time teaching.

WHERE EMPLOYED

Most professional musicians work in large cities, principally in New York, Chicago, and Los Angeles, where most of the Nation's entertainment activities are concentrated. In addition, sizable numbers work in Baltimore, Boston, Cincinnati, Cleveland, Minneapolis, Philadelphia, Rochester, San Francisco, and other cities which have major symphony orchestras or music schools and conservatories. Music teachers in elementary and secondary schools, as well as in colleges and universities, are employed all over the country. Moreover, just about every town and city has at least one private music teacher, usually a pianist. Dance bands and civic orchestras are also located in many communities, although in the smaller towns, their members are usually only part-time musicians with other regular jobs.

A few musicians were employed in hospitals, to work in the field of music therapy, and some worked in music libraries and other places.

TRAINING AND OTHER QUALIFICATIONS

Most people who become professional musicians begin studying an instrument at an early age. Boys and girls often get their first introduction to instrumental music through group instruction in piano, violin, trombone, and other instruments offered in many elementary schools and high schools. They can also take music lessons from private teachers or in the preparatory department of a music conservatory.

To achieve a career as a performer of classical music or as a music teacher, young people need intensive training — either through private study with an accomplished artist, or in a college or university with a strong music program, or in a conservatory of music. They need to acquire not only great technical skill but also a thorough knowledge of music. Before a young person can qualify for advanced study in a music conservatory, it is frequently necessary to have an audition. Many of the teachers in these schools are accomplished artists who will undertake the training only of promising young musicians. An audition is sometimes required also for admission to the department or school of music of a college or university. However, the emphasis on talent as a performer is less for young people preparing to be music teachers than for those preparing only for careers as performers.

Many conservatories of music and college and university schools of music offer 4-year programs leading to a bachelor's degree in music education. Students who complete these programs can qualify for the State certificate required for elementary and secondary school positions. Conservatories and collegiate music schools frequently award also the degree of bachelor of music to students who major in instrumental or vocal music. The 4-year program leading to this degree provides not only training as a performer but also a broad background in musical history and theory, together with some liberal arts courses. Advanced degrees are usually required for college teaching positions, but exceptions may be made for especially well-qualified artists.

Musicians who play jazz and other popular music also must be skilled in their instrument and have an understanding of and feeling for that style of music. As a rule, when young, they take lessons with private teachers and then seize all opportunities, beginning while they are still in high school, to play in amateur or professional performances. Some groups of young people form their own small dance bands. As they gain experience and become known, the players may have opportunities to audition for other local bands and, still later, for the better known bands and orchestras.

EMPLOYMENT OUTLOOK

As a field of employment, instrumental music has been overcrowded for many years, and it is expected to remain so throughout the 1960's. Opportunities for concerts and recitals are not numerous enough to provide adequate employment for all the pianists, violinists, and other instrumentalists qualified as concert artists. Competition is usually keen for positions which afford some stability of employment — for example, jobs with major orchestras and teaching positions in conservatories and colleges and universities. Because of the ease with which a musician can enter private music teaching, the number of music teachers has been and will probably continue to be more than sufficient to give instruction to all the young people seeking lessons. Though many opportunities for single and short-term engagements playing popular music in night clubs, theaters, and other places can be expected, the supply of qualified musicians seeking such jobs is likely to remain greater than the demand. On the other hand, a shortage of highly qualified church organists and choir masters may persist in many communities during the next few years; first-class, experienced accompanists and well trained, outstanding players of stringed instruments, including violin, viola, cello, and double bass, are likely to remain relatively scarce; and public school systems will probably continue to need more, fully qualified music teachers and supervisors.

Employment opportunities for performers are not expected to increase over the long run. Although the number of civic orchestras in smaller communities has been growing steadily, many of these orchestras provide only part-time employment for musicians who work chiefly as teachers or in other occupations. Moreover, the openings created by the establishment of these orchestras have been more than offset by the decline in opportunities in the theater and other places, which has resulted, in part, from the greatly increased use of recorded music.

The employment outlook in music education, for people who are well-qualified as both musicians and as teachers, is considerably brighter than for performers. A great increase in the numbers of young people of high school and college age will take place during the 1960's. Moreover, the number of schools with music programs is growing steadily, and interest in music as an avocation is also rising, as evidenced by the increasing sales of musical instruments. Thus over the long run, a fairly rapid increase can be expected in the employment of elementary and secondary school music teachers and also in the teaching staffs of college and university music schools and conservatories of music.

EARNINGS AND WORKING CONDITIONS

Musicians who were members of the 26 major symphony orchestras in the United States in 1962, had a very wide range of earnings — from a low of $1,600 for the season, to $10,000 and higher. According to the American Symphony Orchestra League, Inc., the average of the salaries paid to musicians by these orchestras was about $4,500 for the season. Those who played in dance bands were paid from $60 to $300 per week in 1962, according to the limited information available. Symphony orchestras had relatively short seasons, generally ranging from 22 to 32 weeks a year. Instrumentalists who were members of small ensembles reportedly received as much as $200 per concert. Concert soloists have the highest earnings of all musicians, but they have to deduct the cost of expensive clothes, travel, and management and coaching fees from their earnings. The amount they receive for a performance depends to a large extent on their professional reputations.

The salaries of public school music teachers are determined by the salary schedule adopted for all teachers. . . . However, they frequently supplement their earnings by giving private music lessons and taking church positions. Earnings from private teaching are very uncertain and vary according to the musician's reputation, the number of teachers in the locality, the number of students desiring lessons, the economic status of the community, and other factors.

Musicians who are performers customarily work at night and on weekends. They must also spend considerable time in regular daily practice and in rehearsing new scores. Most private teaching is done in the late afternoon, on Saturdays, and sometimes in the evening.

Performers may have relatively long periods of unemployment between jobs and, thus, the overall level of their earnings is generally lower than that in many other occupations. Moreover, performers do not usually work steadily for one employer. Consequently, few performers can qualify for unemployment compensation, and they seldom have either sick leave or vacations with pay.

Most musicians who play professionally belong to the American Federation of Musicians (AFL–CIO). Concert soloists also belong to the American Guild of Musical Artists, Inc. (AFL–CIO).

WHERE TO GO FOR MORE INFORMATION

Information about wages, hours of work, and working conditions for professional musicians is available from:

American Federation of Musicians (AFL–CIO),
425 Park Ave., New York, N.Y., 10022.

Information about employment opportunities for church musicians, as well as the requirements for certification of organists and choir masters, may be secured from:

American Guild of Organists,
630 Fifth Ave., New York, N.Y., 10020.

A list of accredited schools of music is available from:

National Association of Schools of Music,
Knox College, Galesburg, Ill., 61401.

Further information about music teaching in elementary and secondary schools is available from:

Music Educators National Conference,
The National Education Association of the United States,
1201 16th St. N.W., Washington, D.C., 20036.

Information about employment opportunities with symphony orchestras may be obtained from:

The American Symphony Orchestra League, Inc.,
Symphony Hill, P.O. Box 66, Vienna, Va., 22180.

SINGERS AND SINGING TEACHERS

NATURE OF WORK

Professional singing is an art which requires not only a fine voice, but also a highly developed technique and a broad knowledge of music. The pinnacle of a singing career is to become an opera and concert star. The tiny group of famous artists who have reached this height sing leading roles with the major opera companies, go on concert tours in the United States and other countries, and often make recordings. Somewhat larger numbers of singers obtain secondary roles in operas and engagements as soloists in oratorios and other types of performances. A much larger group — probably the majority of all professional singers of classical music — are soloists in churches or synagogues. Some singers also become members of opera and musical comedy choruses or other professional choral groups.

Singers who specialize in popular music have a style of singing so different from that of singers of classical music that the two groups have little in common technically. Although most popular music singers have some vocal training, many of them rely on their personalities to a much greater extent than do singers of classical music to help them "put a song across." Popular music singers perform in musical shows of all kinds — in the movies, on the stage, on radio and television, and in nightclubs and other entertainment places. They may be employed as featured singers with a dance band; or they may sing with other vocalists in small groups such as trios or quartets. The best known popular music singers make many recordings.

Since most singers of both classical and popular music have only part-time or irregular employment as singers, they often have full-time jobs of other types and sing only in the evenings or on weekends. Some — chiefly singers of serious music — give private voice lessons. A sizable number of singers with the necessary qualifications are employed in elementary and secondary schools, where they teach music appreciation courses and lead choruses. Others give voice training or direct choral or opera theater groups in music conservatories or in colleges and universities with schools or departments of music.

WHERE EMPLOYED

Probably not more than 75,000 to 80,000 people were earning the major part of their incomes from singing engagements or vocal teaching in 1962. Opportunities for singing engagements are mainly in New York City, Los Angeles, and Chicago — the Nation's chief entertainment centers. Nashville, Tenn., is a major place of employment for singers, including those who specialize in folk and country music, for both "live" performances and recordings. Persons trained as singers who teach music in elementary and secondary schools and in colleges, universities, and conservatories of music are employed throughout the country. Opportunities for part-time employment, chiefly as church singers, are to be found in small towns as well as in big cities.

TRAINING AND OTHER QUALIFICATIONS

Young people who want to perform professionally as singers of serious, or classical, music should acquire a broad background in music, including its theory and history. The ability to dance is also very helpful since singers who perform in musical comedies and other shows are frequently required to dance as well as to sing. In addition, boys and girls interested in a singing career should start piano lessons at an early age. As a rule, voice training should not begin until after the individual has matured physically, although young boys who sing in church choirs receive some training before their voices change. Moreover, because of the work and expense involved in serious voice training — which often continues for years after the singer's professional career has started — it is important that a prospective singer audition before a competent voice teacher to determine whether professional training is warranted.

Young people can prepare for careers as singers of classical music by enrolling in a music conservatory, a school or department of music connected with a college or university, or by taking private voice lessons. Before students are admitted to music conservatories or to college- or university-connected schools or departments of music, they may have to audition before a faculty member who may be a well-known artist. These schools provide not only voice training but other training necessary for understanding and interpreting music, including music-related training in foreign languages, and sometimes dramatic training. After completing a 4-year course of study, a graduate may be awarded either the degree of Bachelor of Music or Bachelor of Science (in music) or Bachelor of Fine Arts.

Young singers who plan to teach music in public elementary or secondary schools need at least a bachelor's degree with a major in music education and must meet their State certification requirements for teachers. Such training is available in over 500 colleges and universities throughout the country. College teachers are usually required to have a master's degree and sometimes a doctor's degree, but exceptions may be made for especially well-qualified artists.

Although voice training is an asset for singers of popular music, many with untrained voices have had successful careers. The typical popular song does not demand that the voice be developed to cover as wide a range on the musical scale as is required for classical music, and the lack of a powerful voice may be overcome by using a microphone.

Young singers of popular songs may become known by participating in amateur and paid performances in their communities. These engagements may lead to employment with local dance bands, and possibly later with well-known ones.

In addition to musical ability, it often takes an outstanding personality, an attractive appearance, good contacts, and good luck to achieve a singing career. Furthermore, a career in this art is often relatively short, since it depends on a good voice and public acceptance of the artist, both of which may be affected by age.

EMPLOYMENT OUTLOOK

The employment situation for singers will probably remain highly competitive during the remainder of the 1960's. Competition among popular singers will continue to be especially keen. A great number of single-job openings are likely to occur in the entertainment field — the opera and concert stage, the movies, the theater, nightclubs, radio and television, dance bands, and other places — but not enough to provide steady employment for all qualified singers. The great majority of professional singers, therefore, will probably have to supplement their incomes by working part time as singing teachers or in other jobs. The demand for church singers is expected to expand because of the continued growth in number of religious congregations, but most of these openings will probably be filled either by part-time singers who have steady employment in other fields or by volunteers.

Little growth in overall employment opportunities for performers is likely over the long run. The use of recorded music has practically replaced the "live" singer on radio; also, the number of television performances given by singers is, and will probably continue to be, limited. However, there is a growing demand for singers to record commercials for both radio and television advertising. The outlook for singers who can meet State certification requirements for positions as music teachers or who can qualify for college teaching will be considerably brighter than for performers. As school enrollments increase, the demand for music teachers in the Nation's elementary and secondary schools is expected to grow and some increased employment of music teachers can be expected in colleges and universities also, since enrollments in schools and departments of music in these institutions are likely to rise along with the increase expected in college enrollments generally. In addition, music teachers will be needed to replace those who will transfer to other fields of work, retire, or die.

EARNINGS AND WORKING CONDITIONS

Most professional singers have relatively modest earnings. For example, soloists with church choirs received about $25 per service, or its equivalent each month, in 1962, according to the limited information available. Singers employed by dance bands and in motion pictures earned as much as $200 per week. In contrast, the relatively few well-known singers in the field earn considerably more than these amounts. A concert soloist, opera star, or a top recording artist of popular music may command more than $1,000 for a single performance.

The salaries of public school music teachers are determined by the salary schedule adopted for all teachers in their school system. Private music teachers charge fees which vary greatly, depending on the teacher's reputation, the economic status of the families in the community, and other factors.

Singers generally work at night and on week-ends. School teachers have regular working hours, and private voice teachers can usually give lessons at their own convenience. Work in the entertainment field is seasonal, and few performers have steady jobs.

Singers who perform professionally on the concert stage or in opera belong to the American Guild of Musical Artists, Inc.; those who sing on radio or television or who make phonograph recordings are members of the American Federation of Television and Radio Artists; singers in the variety and night club field belong to the American Guild of Variety Artists; those who sing in musical comedy and operettas belong to the Actors' Equity Association; and those who sing in the movies belong to the Screen Actors Guild, Inc. All of these unions are branches of the Associated Actors and Artistes of America (AFL–CIO).

WHERE TO GO FOR MORE INFORMATION

Information about wages, hours of work, and working conditions for performers is available from the unions which organize singers in the various entertainment media.

Information about accredited schools and departments of music may be obtained from:

National Association of Schools of Music,
Knox College, Galesburg, Ill., 61401.

Further information about music teaching in elementary and secondary schools is available from:

Music Educators National Conference,
The National Education Association of the United States,
1201 16th St. N.W., Washington, D.C., 20036.

Appendix B

LIST OF MEMBERS OF THE MUSIC PUBLISHERS' ASSOCIATION OF THE UNITED STATES

ABINGDON PRESS
(Methodist Publishing House)
201 – 8th Avenue South
Nashville 3, Tennessee

ASSOCIATED MUSIC PUBLISHERS, INC.
609 Fifth Avenue
New York, New York 10017

C. L. BARNHOUSE COMPANY
110 B Avenue East
Oskaloosa, Iowa

BELWIN, INC.
250 Maple Avenue
Rockville Centre, New York

BENNER PUBLISHERS
1739 Randolph Road
Schenectady, New York 12308

THE BIG THREE MUSIC CORPORATION
1540 Broadway
New York, New York 10036

BOOSEY AND HAWKES, INC.
30 West 57th Street
New York, New York 10019

BOURNE COMPANY
136 West 52nd Street
New York, New York 10019

BREGMAN, VOCCO & CONN, INC.
1619 Broadway
New York, New York 10019

BRODT MUSIC COMPANY
Box 1207
Charlotte, North Carolina 28201

CANYON PRESS, INC.
17 Kearney Street
East Orange, New Jersey 07017

CHAPPELL & CO., INC.
609 Fifth Avenue
New York, New York 10017

CHANTRY MUSIC PRESS, INC.
32-34 Center Street
Springfield, Ohio 45501

GEORGE M. COHAN MUSIC
PUBLISHING CO.
1776 Broadway
New York, New York 10019

M. M. COLE PUBLISHING COMPANY
251 E. Grand Ave.
Chicago, Illinois 60611

FRANCO COLOMBO, INC.
16 West 61st Street
New York, New York

CONCORDIA MUSIC PUBLISHING
HOUSE
3558 South Jefferson Avenue
St. Louis, Missouri 63118

PIETRO DEIRO PUBLICATIONS
133 Seventh Avenue South
New York, New York 10014

ELKAN-VOGEL COMPANY, INC.
1712 Sansom Street
Philadelphia, Pennsylvania 19103

CARL FISCHER, INC.
62 Cooper Square
New York, New York 10003

J. FISCHER & BRO.
Harristown Road
Glen Rock, New Jersey 07452

HAROLD FLAMMER, INC.
251 West 19th Street
New York, New York 10011

CHARLES FOLEY, INC.
67 West 44th Street
New York, New York 10036

SAM FOX PUBLISHING CO., INC.
11 West 60th Street
New York, New York 10023

FRANK MUSIC CORP.
119 West 57th Street
New York, New York 10019

GALAXY MUSIC CORP.
2121 Broadway
New York, New York 10023

GAMUT COMPANY
P.O. Box 6600
Fort Worth, Texas

DAVID GORNSTON
117 West 48th Street
New York, New York 10036

THE H. W. GRAY COMPANY, INC.
159 East 48th Street
New York, New York 10017

NEIL KJOS MUSIC COMPANY
525 Busse Highway
Park Ridge, Illinois

LEBLANC PUBLICATIONS, INC.
7019 30th Avenue
Kenosha, Wisconsin

LEEDS MUSIC CORP.
445 Park Avenue
New York, New York 10036

LORENZ PUBLISHING COMPANY
501 E. Third Street
Dayton, Ohio 45401

EDWARD B. MARKS MUSIC CORP.
136 West 52nd Street
New York, New York 10019

McLAUGHLIN & REILLY
252 Huntington Avenue
Boston, Massachusetts 02115

MEL BAY PUBLICATIONS, INC.
133 West Jefferson
Kirkwood 22, Missouri

MERCURY MUSIC CORPORATION
17 West 60th Street
New York, New York

MILLS MUSIC, INC.
1619 Broadway
New York, New York

EDWIN H. MORRIS & CO., INC.
31 West 54th Street
New York, New York 10019

MUSICORD PUBLICATIONS
1871 Victory Boulevard
Staten Island, New York 10314

OXFORD UNIVERSITY PRESS
417 Fifth Avenue
New York, New York 10016

J. W. PEPPER & SON, INC.
231 North Third Street
Philadelphia, Pennsylvania

C. F. PETERS CORP.
373 Park Avenue South
New York, New York 10016

THEODORE PRESSER COMPANY
Presser Place
Bryn Mawr, Pennsylvania

REPERTOIRE MUSIC, INC.
29 Chestnut Street
Ridgewood, New Jersey

RUBANK, INC.
5544 West Armstrong Avenue
Chicago, Illinois 60646

E. C. SCHIRMER MUSIC COMPANY
600 Washington Street
Boston, Massachusetts

G. SCHIRMER, INC.
609 Fifth Avenue
New York, New York 10017

SCHMITT, HALL & McCREARY CO.
Park Avenue at Sixth Street
Minneapolis 15, Minnesota

SHAPIRO BERNSTEIN & CO., INC.
666 Fifth Avenue
New York. New York 10019

SHAWNEE PRESS, INC.
Delaware Water Gap, Pennsylvania

SOUTHERN MUSIC COMPANY
1100 Broadway
San Antonio, Texas 78206

SOUTHERN MUSIC PUBLISHING
COMPANY
1619 Broadway
New York, New York 10019

SUMMY-BIRCHARD COMPANY
1834 Ridge Avenue
Evanston, Illinois

WORLD LIBRARY OF SACRED
MUSIC, INC.
2145 Central Parkway
Cincinnati, Ohio 45214

Appendix C

LIST OF MEMBER ORGANIZATIONS IN NATIONAL MUSIC COUNCIL

AMATEUR CHAMBER MUSIC PLAYERS
Samuel P. Hayes, Jr., Chairman
Helen Rice, Secretary
15 West 67th Street, New York, N.Y. 10023

AMERICAN ACADEMY OF TEACHERS
OF SINGING
Homer G. Mowe, Chairman
171 West 71st Street, New York, N.Y. 10023

AMERICAN CHORAL DIRECTORS
ASSOCIATION
J. Clark Rhodes, President
University of Tennessee, Knoxville, Tenn.

AMERICAN CHORAL FOUNDATION
B. L. Jessup, Jr., Administrative Director
101 West 31st Street, New York, N.Y. 10001

AMERICAN COMPOSERS ALLIANCE
Richard Donovan, President
157 Armory Street, New Haven, Conn.

AMERICAN FEDERATION OF
MUSICIANS
Herman D. Kenin, President
641 Lexington Avenue, New York, N.Y.

AMERICAN GUILD OF AUTHORS AND
COMPOSERS
Burton Lane, President
50 West 57th Street, New York, N.Y. 10019

AMERICAN GUILD OF MUSICAL
ARTISTS
John Brownlee, President
1841 Broadway, New York, N.Y. 10023

AMERICAN GUILD OF ORGANISTS
Alec Wyton, President
630 Fifth Avenue, New York, N.Y. 10020

AMERICAN MATTHAY ASSOCIATION
Mrs. Helen Parker Ford, President
66 Milbank Avenue, Greenwich, Conn.

AMERICAN MUSIC CENTER
Hugo Weisgall, President
2109 Broadway, New York, N.Y. 10023

AMERICAN MUSIC CONFERENCE
James L. Bixby, Executive Vice-President
332 South Michigan Avenue
Chicago, Ill. 60604

AMERICAN MUSICOLOGICAL SOCIETY
William J. Mitchell, President
Music Department
Columbia University, New York, N.Y. 10027

AMERICAN SOCIETY OF COMPOSERS,
AUTHORS AND PUBLISHERS
Stanley Adams, President
575 Madison Avenue, New York, N.Y. 10022

AMERICAN SOCIETY OF MUSIC
ARRANGERS
M. Russel Goudey, President
224 West 49th Street, New York, N.Y.

AMERICAN STRING TEACHERS
ASSOCIATION
Paul Rolland, President
University of Illinois, Urbana, Ill. 61803

AMERICAN SYMPHONY ORCHESTRA
LEAGUE
Mrs. Helen M. Thompson, Executive
Vice-President
Box 66, Vienna, Va.

BROADCAST MUSIC, INC.
Robert B. Sour, President
589 Fifth Avenue, New York, N.Y. 10017

COLLEGE BAND DIRECTORS
NATIONAL ASSOCIATION
Manley Whitcomb, President
Florida State University, Tallahassee, Fla.

COLLEGE MUSIC SOCIETY
Henry Kaufman, President
Rutgers Univ., New Brunswick, N.J.

COMPOSERS AND LYRICISTS GUILD
OF AMERICA
Kenneth Thomson, Executive Director
9157 Sunset Blvd., #204
Los Angeles, Calif. 90069

DELTA OMICRON
Helen D. Bishop, President
51–3 Revere Road, Drexel Hill, Pa.

HYMN SOCIETY OF AMERICA
Rev. Deane Edwards, President
475 Riverside Drive, New York, N.Y. 10027

INSTITUTE OF JAZZ STUDIES
Marshall Stearns, President
108 Waverly Place, New York, N.Y.

LEAGUE OF COMPOSERS AND
INTERNATIONAL SOCIETY FOR
CONTEMPORARY MUSIC, U.S. BRANCH
Felix Greissle, Executive Secretary
Marks Music Co., 136 W. 52nd St.
New York, N.Y. 10019

LESCHETIZKY ASSOCIATION
Edwine Behre, President
162 West 54th Street, New York, N.Y. 10019

MORAVIAN MUSIC FOUNDATION
Ewald V. Nolte, Director
Salem Station, Winston-Salem, N.C.

MU PHI EPSILON
Janet Adams Wilkie, President
5744 34th St., N.E. Seattle, Wash. 98105

MUSIC COMMITTEE OF THE
PEOPLE-TO-PEOPLE PROGRAM
Mrs. Jouett Shouse, Chairman
1701 Pennsylvania Ave., N.W., Rm. 500
Washington, D.C.

MUSIC EDUCATORS NATIONAL
CONFERENCE
Paul Van Bodegraven, President
New York University, Washington Square
New York, N.Y.
Vanett Lawler, Executive Secretary
1201 Sixteenth St., N.W.
Washington, D.C. 20036

MUSIC LIBRARY ASSOCIATION
Irving Lowens, President
Music Div., Library of Congress
Washington, D.C. 20540

MUSIC PUBLISHERS' ASSOCIATION
OF THE UNITED STATES
Don Malin, Marks Music Corp.
136 West 52nd Street, New York, N.Y., 10019

MUSIC TEACHERS NATIONAL
ASSOCIATION
Willis F. Ducrest, President
University of Southwestern Louisiana
Lafayette, La.
G. W. Fahrer, Jr., Executive Secretary
2209 Carew Tower, Cincinnati 2, Ohio

NATIONAL ASSOCIATION FOR
AMERICAN COMPOSERS AND
CONDUCTORS
Herman Neuman, President
Station WNYC, Municipal Bldg.
New York, N.Y.

NATIONAL ASSOCIATION OF
MUSIC MERCHANTS
William R. Gard, Executive Secretary
222 West Adams Street, Rm. 316
Chicago, Ill. 60606

NATIONAL ASSOCIATION FOR
MUSIC THERAPY
Dr. Leo C. Muskatvec
Milwaukee Co. Mental Health Center
Milwaukee, Wis.

NATIONAL ASSOCIATION OF SCHOOLS
OF MUSIC
C. B. Hunt, Jr., President
George Peabody College, Nashville, Tenn.
Warren A. Scharf, Executive Secretary
1501 New Hampshire Ave., N.W.
Washington, D.C. 20036

NATIONAL ASSOCIATION OF
TEACHERS OF SINGING
William Vennard, President
University of Southern California
Los Angeles, Calif. 90007

NATIONAL CATHOLIC MUSIC
EDUCATORS ASSOCIATION
Rev. Eugene Lindusky, OSC
Crosier Seminary, Onamia, Minnesota 56359

NATIONAL FEDERATION OF
MUSIC CLUBS
Mrs. Clifton J. Muir, President
3804 Alhambra Circle, Coral Gables, Fla.

NATIONAL GUILD OF COMMUNITY
MUSIC SCHOOLS
Robert F. Egan, President
504-D Grand Street, New York, N.Y. 10002

NATIONAL GUILD OF PIANO
TEACHERS
Irl Allison, Jr., President
Box 1807, Austin, Texas 78767

NATIONAL MUSIC CAMP
Joseph E. Maddy, President
Interlochen, Mich.

NATIONAL MUSIC PUBLISHERS'
ASSOCIATION, INC.
Leonard Feist, Executive Secretary
460 Park Avenue
New York, N.Y.

NATIONAL OPERA ASSOCIATION
Robert Gay, President
Northwestern University, Evanston, Ill.

NATIONAL PIANO MANUFACTURERS
ASSOCIATION OF AMERICA
G. M. Otto, Executive Secretary
435 N. Michigan Avenue, Chicago, Ill. 60611

PHI BETA
Mrs. Stanley H. Frohmader, President
514 LeRoy Road, Madison, Wisc. 53704

PHI MU ALPHA SINFONIA
Harry R. Wilson, President
Teachers College, Columbia University
New York, N.Y. 10027
Price Doyle, Secretary-Treasurer
Murray State College, Murray, Ky.

PIANO TECHNICIANS GUILD
James H. Burton, Executive Secretary
512 First Avenue North, Seattle, Wash. 98109

PI KAPPA LAMBDA
George Howerton, President
Northwestern University, Evanston, Ill.

RECORD INDUSTRY ASSOCIATION
OF AMERICA
Henry Brief, Executive Secretary
One East 57th Street, New York, N.Y. 10022

SIGMA ALPHA IOTA
Mrs. James G. Kirk, President
7906 Jamieson Avenue, Reseda, Calif. 91335

SOCIETY FOR ETHNOMUSICOLOGY
David P. McAllester, President
Wesleyan University, Middletown, Conn.

SOCIETY FOR THE PRESERVATION AND
ENCOURAGEMENT OF BARBER SHOP
QUARTET SINGING IN AMERICA
Barie Best, Executive Director
6315 Third Avenue, Kenosha, Wisc.

SOCIETY FOR THE PUBLICATION OF
AMERICAN MUSIC
Luther Noss, President
Yale University, New Haven, Conn.

UNITED STATES ARMY, NAVY AND
AIR FORCE BANDSMEN'S ASSOCIATION
Capt. A. R. Teta, Secretary
P.O. Box 1826, New Haven, Conn.

Appendix D

LIST OF CONCERT MANAGEMENTS
UNDER AGMA AGREEMENTS

HERBERT BARRETT
250 West 57th St., New York City 19

BERNARD MANAGEMENT BUREAU
242 W. 76 St., New York 23

COLBERT ARTISTS MANAGEMENT
850 Seventh Avenue, Penthouse A
New York City 19

COLUMBIA ARTISTS
MANAGEMENT INC.
(including Community Concerts)
165 West 57 Street, New York City 19

DIANNE COPELON
382 Central Park West, N.Y.C.

CRAWFORD PRODUCTIONS
166 West 72nd Street, N.Y.C.

GIORGIO D'ANDRIA
1005 Carnegie Hall, New York City 19

ELWOOD EMERICK
501 Madison Avenue, N.Y.C. 22

JOHN B. FISHER
253 West 72nd Street, N.Y.C. 23

LOUISE FLAVEL
155 West 68 St., New York City

JULE FOSTER ASSOCIATES, LTD.
41 Central Park West, N.Y.C.

THE FRIEDBERG MANAGEMENT
111 West 57 Street, New York City 19

ROBERT GARDNER MANAGEMENT
119 W. 57 St., N.Y.C.

GENERAL ARTISTS CORPORATION
640 Fifth Avenue, New York City 19

ROBERT M. GEWALD
Suite 1530, 2 W. 59 St., N.Y.C.

SIEGFRIED HEARST
344 West 72nd St., New York City 23

HANS J. HOFMANN
200 West 58th Street, N.Y.C.

HUROK ATTRACTIONS, INC.
730 Fifth Ave., New York City 19

JUDSON, O'NEILL, BEALL &
STEINWAY, INC.
119 W. 57 St., N.Y.C. 19

ALBERT KAY ASSOCIATES
38 West 53 St., N.Y.C. 19

LUDWIG LUSTIG
111 West 57th St., New York City 19

MEYER MANAGEMENT CORPORATION
111 West 57 Street, New York City 19

WILLIAM MORRIS AGENCY
1740 Broadway, New York City 19

JERRY MERTON AGENCY, INC.
9056 Santa Monica Blvd., Los Angeles, Calif.

MUSICAL ARTISTS (SUSAN PIMSLEUR)
119 West 57th St., New York City 19

EMMY NICLAS
147 West 55th St., New York City 19

FELIX W. SALMAGGI ASSOCIATES
1860 Broadway, New York City 23

JAMES SARDOS MANAGEMENT CORP.
180 West End Ave., New York City

JIM SCOVOTTI ASSOCIATES
200 W. 57 St., New York City 19

ERIC SEMON ASSOCIATES
31 West 57 Street, New York 19, N.Y.

MILDRED SHAGAL, INC.
119 West 57 Street, New York City

SEYMOUR SOKOLOFF
545 St. Charles Ave., New Orleans 12, La.

WILLIAM L. STEIN, INC.
113 West 57th St., New York City 19

GRETA STROK
25 East 67th Street, N.Y.C.

ANN SUMMERS MANAGEMENT
135 W. 56th St., N.Y.C.

SUMMY-BIRCHARD COMPANY
Concert & Artists Division
31 West 57th St., N.Y.C. 19

THEATRICAL ASSOCIATES
909 North 1st St., Phoenix, Arizona

CHARLES B. TRANUM, INC.
603 Madison Avenue, N.Y.C.

ARN VACCHINA ASSOCIATES
The Westover
253 West 72nd Street, N.Y.C. 23

VINCENT ATTRACTIONS, INC.
119 West 57th St., New York City 19

CONSTANCE WARDLE
360 West 55th St., New York City 19

RUTH WEBB
1650 Broadway, N.Y.C.

HENRY WILLIAM WIESE
1674 Broadway, N.Y.C.

RONALD WILFORD ASSOCIATES, INC.
165 West 57 Street, New York City 19

CARL YOST
344 West 72nd St., New York City 23

ALFRED ZEGA
250 West 57th St., New York City 19

Appendix E

FORM OF STANDARD AGMA ARTIST-MANAGER AGREEMENT

This contract is between_____
(hereinafter called "MANAGER"), located at_____
_____and_____
_____(hereinafter called "ARTIST") whose residence or
usual place of business is_____

1. ARTIST hereby appoints MANAGER as his sole and exclusive manager and personal representative in all branches of the entertainment industry in the United States and Canada, except the legitimate stage, motion pictures, television, lectures and the variety field, and MANAGER hereby accepts such appointment.

2. ARTIST warrants that he is a member of AGMA in good standing or will become so pursuant to Rule "C" on the reverse side hereof, and agrees to remain in good standing throughout the term hereof.

3. The term of this contract shall commence the_____
day of_____, _____, and end the_____day of
_____, _____. ARTIST grants MANAGER an option to extend the term of this contract upon the same terms for an additional_____( ) year, commencing upon the first day subsequent to the day that the term of this contract would otherwise expire. In the event that such option is exercised, ARTIST grants MANAGER an additional option further to extend the term of this contract upon the same terms for an additional _____( ) year, commencing upon the first day subsequent to the day that the term of this contract, as theretofore extended, would otherwise expire. In the event that such additional option is exercised, ARTIST grants MANAGER a second additional option further to extend the term of this contract upon the same terms for an additional_____ ( ) year, commencing upon the first day subsequent to the day that the term of this contract, as therefore extended, would otherwise expire. In each instance that MANAGER shall elect to exercise any option contained in this paragraph, MANAGER shall give or mail to ARTIST notice not later than the December 1st next preceding the expiration of the then term of this contract, and upon such notice being given or mailed the term of this contract shall be so extended.

4. MANAGER is hereby appointed as the attorney-in-fact for ARTIST to execute in ARTIST's behalf contracts for the personal services of ARTIST in the branches of the entertainment field covered by this contract.

For Regular Concert Engagements, the Minimum Fee shall be_____$_____
per engagement

For Symphony Orchestra Engagements, the Minimum Fee shall be $_____
per engagement

For Civic, Community and Similarly Organized Concert Engagements, the Net Minimum Fee (after deduction of "differential") shall be $_____
per engagement

5. (a) In consideration of the performance by MANAGER of the terms of this contract ARTIST agrees to pay MANAGER the following percentages of the gross earnings of ARTIST as herein defined.

Regular Concert Engagements Including Symphony Orchestra and Oratorio _____%
(not more than 20%)

Civic, Community and Similarly Organized Concert Engagements_____ _____%
(not more than 15%)

Radio Engagements, including electrical transcriptions_____ _____%
(not more than 10%)

Operatic Engagements and Ballet Engagements (other than concerts)_____ _____%
(not more than 10%)

Phonograph Records_____ _____%
(not more than 10%)

(b) MANAGER shall use his best efforts to collect for ARTIST and in ARTIST's behalf all monies which may become due to ARTIST for engagements performed by ARTIST on which MANAGER shall be entitled to commissions hereunder. MANAGER shall pay to ARTIST net balances due to ARTIST from all funds received in ARTIST's behalf, at thirty (30) day intervals, accompanied by a written statement showing how such net balances were arrived at, unless ARTIST shall request otherwise.

6. (a) ARTIST agrees that he will conscientiously fulfill all engagements contracted for by MANAGER in behalf of ARTIST, pursuant to this contract except as provided in Rule "H" on the reverse side hereof.

(b) ARTIST will promptly turn over to MANAGER all inquiries with reference to his services in all branches of the entertainment industry covered by the terms of this contract.

(c) ARTIST will be responsible for all traveling, hotel and all other non-booking expenses whatsoever of ARTIST and his accompanist as well as accompanist's salary.

(d) ARTIST shall pay for all of his normal promotional expenses incurred by himself or MANAGER.

7. ALL OF THE PROVISIONS ON THE REVERSE SIDE OF THIS CONTRACT SHALL BE DEEMED INCORPORATED HEREIN WITH THE SAME FORCE AND EFFECT AS THOUGH THEY PRECEDED THE SIGNATURES HERETO AFFIXED.

IN WITNESS WHEREOF, the parties hereto have executed this contract in triplicate as of the_____day of_____, 196

_____   By:_____
               ARTIST   (Title)_____

RULES

A. ARTIST warrants that he has no contract for management and personal representation which is inconsistent with the terms of this contract.

B. MANAGER warrants that he has executed the AMERICAN GUILD OF MUSICAL ARTISTS, INC. (AGMA) — MANAGERS BASIC AGREEMENT. MANAGER represents and warrants that he is organized and equipped to render capable and efficient services for ARTIST in all branches of the entertainment industry covered by this contract and will continue to be so equipped throughout the balance of the term hereof; that he will use his best efforts in furthering the career of ARTIST and, incidentally, in assisting ARTIST in procuring engagements and that he will, at the request of ARTIST, counsel and advise ARTIST in matters which concern ARTIST's professional interests in the fields covered by this contract; and that MANAGER will maintain an adequate organization to serve ARTIST during the term of this contract.

C. In the event that ARTIST is not presently a member of AGMA in good standing, ARTIST agrees either

I. to become a member of AGMA in good standing, immediately after his first public appearance in the United States or Canada after the date hereof, and to remain in good standing throughout the balance of the term hereof; or

II. if ARTIST is not within continental United States at the time of the execution of this contract, to become a member of AGMA in good standing within thirty (30) days after the arrival of ARTIST in continental United States or Canada or, in any event, immediately after the first public appearance of ARTIST in continental United States after the date hereof and to remain in good standing throughout the balance of the term hereof.

D. As used in Paragraph "3", the phrase "the same terms" shall not mean that ARTIST grants MANAGER any additional options to extend the term of this contract, and no additional options shall be effective unless in writing signed by ARTIST.

E. In the event that ARTIST shall, for any reason whatsoever, breach any term set forth in Paragraph "2" of this contract subsequent to the execution hereof, and AGMA shall, by written notice, require MANAGER to terminate the term of this contract, MANAGER shall have the right to terminate the term of this contract immediately upon giving ARTIST notice thereof; provided, however, that MANAGER shall have the right, which shall be stated in said notice, to continue to represent ARTIST and to receive commissions with respect to such engagements as were secured prior to receipt by MANAGER of said written notice from AGMA.

F. In the case of the fields specifically enumerated in Paragraph "4", no contract shall provide for payment to ARTIST of a lesser fee than is therein set forth, unless ARTIST shall have approved such lesser fee in advance. In the case of the fields not specifically enumerated in Paragraph "4", no commitment shall be made by MANAGER until there has been mutual agreement between ARTIST and MANAGER as to fee, date, place of engagement, time of engagement and, in the case of radio engagements, sponsor.

G. "Gross earnings" of ARTIST as referred to in Paragraph "5", shall consist of all money and other consideration (a) received by ARTIST directly or indirectly from engagements covered by this contract performed during the term or extended term hereof, (b) received by ARTIST directly or indirectly from engagements covered by Paragraph VII (g) of AGMA-MANAGERS BASIC AGREEMENT performed subsequent to the expiration of the term or extended term hereof, (c) stipulated in contracts as and for ARTIST's fee for engagements providing for performances during the periods specified in (a) or (b) above but which ARTIST, without just cause, fails to perform, (d) accruing under engagements which are paid to creditors or assignees of ARTIST or are withheld pursuant to law, and (e) monies received in settlement less deductions as stipulated in Paragraph VII (h) of AGMA-MANAGERS BASIC AGREEMENT. Except as to (c) and (d) above, the foregoing shall be payable only when, as and if such monies are received by ARTIST or by anyone on ARTIST's behalf.

H. The exceptions referred to in Paragraph "6 (a)" are as follows:

I. Engagements contracted for by MANAGER after ARTIST shall have given MANAGER ninety (90) days prior notice of ARTIST's unavailability for the date of such engagement, provided, however, that no such notice shall be given during the period commencing January 15th and ending April 15th, in any year during the term or extended term of this contract.
II. Engagements which ARTIST is unable to fulfill due to physical disability, the acts or regulations of public authorities, civil tumult, epidemic, interruption or delay of transportation service, labor difficulties or strikes which are not in violation of Paragraphs IX or III (c) of the AGMA-MANAGERS BASIC AGREEMENT, or any other cause beyond the control of ARTIST.

I. ARTIST grants to MANAGER the right to use and to license others to use the name, likeness and biography of ARTIST for informative purposes and to publicize and advertise ARTIST and ARTIST's engagements. Such use may be in combination with advertising of products or services of any employer of ARTIST, but shall not amount to an endorsement thereof by ARTIST.

J. All membership dues of ARTIST which are payable to AGMA may, upon the written request of AGMA be deducted by MANAGER from the compensation or other monies of ARTIST received by MANAGER and paid by MANAGER directly to AGMA, but the authority granted by this Paragraph J may be revoked by ARTIST giving written notice to MANAGER at any time after one (1) year from the date hereof.

K. Where any contract for ARTIST's services requires that all or any part of ARTIST's fee shall be paid prior to the performance of ARTIST's engagement, MANAGER shall have the right to direct ARTIST to collect such fee or part thereof prior to ARTIST's performance of the engagement; provided, however, that if MANAGER so directs ARTIST and ARTIST fails to perform MANAGER's directions, such failure by ARTIST shall not confer any right on MANAGER with respect to ARTIST nor shall it relieve MANAGER of any of his duties or obligations under this contract.

L. For the purposes of Paragraph 4 of this contract, a pair of symphony orchestral appearances is to be considered as one engagement hereunder, provided that such symphony pair takes place with the same orchestra within three (3) days, it being understood, however, that the symphony pair need not necessarily take place in the same city, provided that one city is the home city of the orchestra, and the other a nearby city.

M. Any and all notices herein provided for shall be in writing, addressed to MANAGER or ARTIST at the address set forth for each of them in this contract, or at such other address as either of them may for himself hereafter in writing designate. Such notices shall be personally delivered, mailed or telegraphed, and if mailed shall be deemed given when enclosed in a properly addressed, postpaid, sealed envelope deposited in a U.S. Post Office or mail box or mail chute maintained by the United States. If telegraphed, such notice shall be deemed to have been given when delivered to the telegraph company.

N. MANAGER agrees that the following persons, and the following persons only: (here the parties may, but need not, insert the names of not more than four (4) persons in MANAGER's employ) shall personally supervise ARTIST's business during the term of this contract. One of such persons shall be available at all reasonable times for consultation with ARTIST in the City in which the office of MANAGER is located as hereinabove set forth. Employees of MANAGER who are not named herein may aid any of the named persons in handling managerial matters for ARTIST. In the event that all the persons above named sever their connections with MANAGER, ARTIST shall have the right within a period of thirty (30) days after the receipt of notice thereof, to terminate the term of this contract.

O. ARTIST shall be or become, and remain during the term of this contract, a member in good standing of all labor organizations having jurisdiction over the services scheduled by MANAGER for ARTIST pursuant to the terms of this contract.

P. ALL OF THE PROVISIONS OF THE AGMA-MANAGERS BASIC AGREEMENT SHALL BE DEEMED INCORPORATED HEREIN WITH THE SAME FORCE AND EFFECT AS THOUGH HEREIN SET FORTH IN FULL. No written or oral waiver by ARTIST of any of the provisions of the said BASIC AGREEMENT or of this contract shall be valid or binding unless the written consent of AGMA with respect to the making of such a waiver is first obtained.

Q. If any provision of this contract or the application of such provision to any person or circumstance, is or shall be or become illegal or invalid, the remainder of this contract, or the application of such provision to persons or circumstances other than those as to which it is held invalid, shall not be affected thereby.

R. This contract cannot be changed orally, and shall be construed, governed and interpreted pursuant to the laws of the State of New York.

S. NOTE: At no time shall ARTIST be bound to MANAGER for a period extending more than four (4) years in the future including all options and rights or renewals exercisable by MANAGER.

T. Further terms not set forth above in this contract may be set forth under Schedule "A" annexed hereto, and any terms so set forth are hereby made a part of this contract. If any such terms are contrary to the terms of the printed portions of this contract or to the terms of the AGMA-MANAGERS BASIC AGREEMENT or are less favorable to ARTIST than the said AGMA-MANAGERS BASIC AGREEMENT, such contrary or less favorable terms shall be void and of no effect.

Appendix F

AMERICAN GUILD OF MUSICAL ARTISTS

(BRANCH OF ASSOCIATED ACTORS AND ARTISTES OF AMERICA)
AFFILIATED WITH A.F.L. — C.I.O.

1841 BROADWAY • NEW YORK 23, N. Y.
COlumbus 5-3687

STANDARD ARTIST'S CONTRACT FOR EMPLOYMENT

FOR USE FOR EMPLOYMENT IN OPERA, CONCERT, RECITAL, BALLET AND DANCE, CHORUS
AND CHOIR, AND FOR OTHER TYPES OF EMPLOYMENT UNDER THE JURISDICTION OF AGMA

Agreement made this ....day of.., 19........,
by and between the undersigned ARTIST, a member in good standing of the AMERICAN GUILD OF MUSICAL ARTISTS,
(hereinafter referred to as "AGMA"), and the undersigned ASSOCIATION (hereinafter referred to as "EMPLOYER" or
"EMPLOYERS").

1. AGREEMENT OF EMPLOYMENT AND COMPENSATION. The EMPLOYER hereby engages the ARTIST to
render services as ....
(Singer, dancer, chorister, stage director, or in other capacity under the jurisdiction of AGMA)
in the company or production known as ....
(Name of Opera Company, Ballet Company, Concert Attraction, etc.)

Cross out Inapplicable Paragraphs A or B

A. ENGAGEMENT ON A PERFORMANCE BASIS
The EMPLOYER hereby engages the ARTIST to render services in the following productions and roles, on the following
dates and for the following compensations:

PRODUCTION	ROLE	DATE OF PERFORMANCE	COMPENSATION	TRANSPORTATION AMOUNT

and the ARTIST hereby accepts such employment upon the terms set forth herein. The employment of the ARTIST under this
Paragraph A shall be non-cancellable.

B. ENGAGEMENT ON A WEEKLY BASIS
The EMPLOYER hereby engages the ARTIST to render services for a PERIOD OF ....WEEK(S), commencing
with the ....day of..................., 19......., and ending the ...., 19........,
and the EMPLOYER hereby guarantees that the ARTIST will receive the compensation hereinafter set forth for the period of
time hereinabove set forth.

C. List below the roles and operas for which the ARTIST is engaged:

PRODUCTION	ROLE	TRANSPORTATION (AMOUNT)

D. The EMPLOYER agrees to pay the ARTIST the sum of $ ....per week during the above stated period
for rendering the services stated above. The ARTIST hereby agrees to accept this employment upon the terms stated herein.
The employment of the ARTIST under paragraph B above shall be non-cancellable and continuous without a lay-off or
interruption.

E. The compensation under paragraphs A and B above shall be "PAY OR PLAY" and all compensation shall be paid
in United States currency (a) prior to the commencement of each single performance or (b) before 6 P.M. on the last day of
each performance week.

F. TRANSPORTATION. It is understood and agreed that the ARTIST'S first-class railroad transportation from
.....................to ....and return, which must be paid for by the EMPLOYER, is not to be
included in the amount of the ARTIST'S compensation, but must be separately stated in this contract by the EMPLOYER.

2. SECURITY DEPOSIT OR BOND. The EMPLOYER MUST, simultaneously with the filing with AGMA of this contract, but in no event less than one week prior to the 1st rehearsal of the company or production hereinabove described in
paragraph 1 hereof, deposit with AGMA a bond, cash or other security as provided in the Basic Agreement.
The EMPLOYER agrees that this contract is not binding upon the ARTIST until such time as the EMPLOYER deposits
a bond, cash or other security as hereinabove provided and the same has been approved by AGMA.

3. DEDUCTIONS. The actual net compensation of the ARTIST shall be set forth herein and there shall be no remis-
sions, rebates, discounts, booking fees, commissions or other payments or deductions whatsoever from the ARTIST'S compensation except such taxes or withholdings as are required by statute, and except further that initiation fees, and deliquent
dues payable to AGMA shall be deducted from the compensation of the ARTIST and paid by the EMPLOYER to AGMA,
and the ARTIST hereby authorizes the EMPLOYER to make such deductions and payments as AGMA directs. The EM-
PLOYER warrants that this clause will be fully and faithfully observed by himself and by any and all of his agents, representatives and employees. Artist may revoke above authority at any time after 1 year from date hereof.

4. AGMA RULES—ARTIST'S OBLIGATIONS TO AGMA. The ARTIST hereby warrants that he is a member of AGMA in good standing and that he will remain so for the duration of this contract and the ARTIST and the EMPLOYER hereby jointly and severally agree that the ARTIST'S obligations hereunder are subject (1) to the ARTIST'S prior obligations to AGMA as a member thereof, and (2) to AGMA's Constitution, By-Laws, and Rules and Regulations as they now exist or as they may hereafter be amended. The EMPLOYER agrees that its obligations under this contract with the ARTIST are subject to the provisions of AGMA's Constitution, By-Laws, and Rules and Regulations as they now exist or as they may hereafter be amended.

The EMPLOYER represents that a Collective Bargaining Agreement (hereinafter referred to as "BASIC AGREEMENT") exists between AGMA and the EMPLOYER. All the provisions of such Basic Agreement and all AGMA Rules as they now exist or as they may hereafter be amended shall be deemed to be included in this contract as an integral part hereof, except to the extent that any provision of this contract which is more favorable to the ARTIST than any conflicting or inconsistent provision of such Basic Agreement or AGMA Rules, in which event such provision in this contract shall prevail. If no such BASIC AGREEMENT exists between the EMPLOYER and AGMA, then this contract shall not be binding upon the ARTIST but shall nevertheless be enforcable against the EMPLOYER at the option of AGMA or the ARTIST.

The EMPLOYER further agrees (1) that he has notice that the ARTIST is a member of AGMA and must obey AGMA RULES, (2) that he will require the ARTIST to remain a member of AGMA in good standing throughout the duration of this contract, and (3) that he will not require the ARTIST to work in any company under his direction, management or control unless every ARTIST under the jurisdiction of AGMA employed in such company is a member of AGMA in good standing and remains so for the duration of his employment and only so long as the EMPLOYER has fully performed and is fully performing the covenants in each and every employment contract entered into, or hereafter during the term hereof entered into, with each and every AGMA member in each and every company operated and/or owned and/or controlled by him or with which he may be in any way connected.

5. NO WAIVERS OR CHANGES ALLOWED—SCHEDULE "A": The EMPLOYER and the ARTIST hereby mutually agree that no riders, changes or alterations of this printed form, and no addition to this printed form under Schedule "A" below, shall be made or agreed to by either the EMPLOYER or the ARTIST without the written consent of AGMA, and the EMPLOYER further agrees that no such rider, change, or alteration shall be required of or deemed binding upon the ARTIST unless approved by AGMA as provided in the Basic Agreement.

Further provisions and agreements not set forth above in the printed portion of this contract may be set forth under Schedule "A" below, subject, however, to the provisions of the preceding paragraph.

The acceptance by the ARTIST of cash, checks, or other forms of payment, or the deposit or retaining of cash, checks or other forms of payment shall in no way affect the right of the ARTIST or of AGMA to insist upon full payment under this contract. The signing by the ARTIST of waivers or releases, or the deposit of checks or money orders under stipulations, letters or other writings that such deposit is in full payment or the like, shall be of no force or effect.

6. REHEARSALS. The maximum number of rehearsal-hours, days and/or weeks, the maximum number of hours of rehearsal per day and/or per week, and all other regulations and restrictions in connection with rehearsals of the type agreed to hereunder which are set forth in AGMA RULES and/or in any BASIC AGREEMENT governing this contract, shall govern rehearsal hereunder and the rate of payment for rehearsals and for any and all overtime rehearsal-hours, days or weeks.

For and in consideration of the employment agreed to above, and in connection therewith, it is agreed that the ARTIST will rehearse for .... commencing with the .... day of .... , 19 ..... ,
(number of days, hours, weeks, etc.)
and the EMPLOYER agrees to pay the ARTIST the sum of $ .... per .... as compensation therefor. (hour, day, week, etc.)

7. DISCRIMINATION FORBIDDEN. The EMPLOYER agrees that it will not discriminate against any ARTIST in compensation, performances, engagements or in its general relationship with any ARTIST, because of any such ARTIST'S activities in behalf of AGMA, nor shall EMPLOYER discriminate against any ARTIST because of his race, color or creed.

8. SEGREGATION. No ARTIST will be required to appear in any theatre or place of performance where discrimination is practiced because of race, color or creed against any: (1) ARTIST or (2) patron, as to admission or seating arrangements.

9 ARBITRATION. The EMPLOYER and the ARTIST hereby jointly and severally agree that any controversy or claim arising out of or relating to this contract or the breach thereof, or any controversy whatsoever between the EMPLOYER and the ARTIST, shall be settled by Arbitration, in accordance with the provisions of the BASIC AGREEMENT and the rules, then obtaining, of the American Arbitration Association (except as may otherwise be provided in AGMA RULES), and judgment upon the award rendered may be entered in the highest Court of the Forum, State or Federal, having jurisdiction.

10. LAWS GOVERNING. This agreement shall be subject to, be construed by, and the right of all parties thereto shall be determined by the Laws of the State of New York, except as may otherwise be provided.

11. LIABILITY. This contract shall be executed by the ARTIST and by the EMPLOYER. If the EMPLOYER or EMPLOYERS or any of them is a corporation, this agreement must be signed by the corporation and by an individual as an individual and not as a corporate officer, and in any event a person signing as an officer, agent or representative of a corporation agrees that his signature hereto binds him as an individual as well as such officer, agent or representative.

IN WITNESS WHEREOF we have executed this agreement as of the date first above set forth.

IMPORTANT All AGMA RULES which are in force at the time this contract is entered into are part hereof. The EMPLOYER and the ARTIST should keep themselves advised of AGMA RULES posted on the bulletin board in the AGMA office. The Basic Agreement between AGMA and the above Employer may contain modifications of the Standard Agreement. Check with AGMA before you sign this contract.	.... **EMPLOYER(s)** Employer(s) Unemployment Insurance Number _____ .... **ARTIST** .... **ADDRESS**

"SCHEDULE "A""   Social Security No. ☐☐☐☐☐☐☐

Appendix G

FORM OF PUBLISHER-COMPOSER SERIOUS MUSIC CONTRACT

AGREEMENT made this_____day of_____, 19   , between

_____of_____

(hereinafter called "Publisher") and_____

jointly and severally (hereinafter called "Composer").

WITNESSETH:

1. Composer hereby sells, assigns, transfers and delivers to Publisher, its successors and assigns, a certain heretofore unpublished original musical composition, and the manuscript and performance materials (if any) thereof, written and composed by Composer, now entitled:

(hereinafter called the "composition"), including the common law property therein, the title words and music thereof, and the right to secure copyright and all extensions and renewals of copyright therein throughout the entire world and to have and to hold the said copyright and all rights of whatsoever nature thereunder.

2. Composer warrants that the composition is his sole, exclusive and original work; that he has full right and power to make this agreement; that there exists no adverse claim to or in the composition; that valid copyright can be secured therein by Publisher; and that neither the composition nor any part thereof infringes upon the title or the literary, musical, personal or property rights of any person, firm or corporation anywhere in the world.

3. Publisher agrees to use reasonable efforts to exploit the composition in accordance with its business judgment and to pay to Composer, in respect of the composition, sums equal to:

(a) Ten percent (10%) of the retail list prices established by Publisher on all copies of all versions of the composition published by it and sold and paid for in the United States and Canada, and one-half (½) of such amount on all such copies sold outside of the United States and Canada and paid for; provided that if the composition is published in a book with other works, such sums shall be prorated according to the number of compositions in such book.

(b) Fifty percent (50%) of all net sums received by Publisher in respect of any and all licenses issued authorizing the manufacture in the United States and Canada of parts of instruments serving to reproduce the composition, or any parts, arrangements, versions, or adaptations thereof mechanically on phonograph records, tapes and similar devices, or authorizing such usage in synchronization with motion pictures.

(c) Fifty percent (50%) of all net sums received by Publisher for the rental in the United States and Canada of materials furnished to Publisher by Composer, and twenty-five percent (25%) of all net sums received by Publisher for the rental in the United States and Canada of materials produced and paid for by Publisher.

(d) Fifty percent (50%) of all net sums received by Publisher from the licensing of public performance of the composition directly by Publisher to the user.

(e) Fifty percent (50%) of all net sums received by Publisher for any grant to another publisher of the right to publish the composition in a book with other works.

(f) Fifty percent (50%) of all net sums received by Publisher in respect of foreign exploitation of the composition by any means, except as hereinabove otherwise provided.

(g) Fifty percent (50%) of all other net sums received by Publisher in the United States and Canada (except as specifically provided for herein).

Composer shall not share in any sum or sums received by Publisher from ASCAP or BMI or any public performing rights organization which pays performance fees directly to composers.

Except as specifically provided in this paragraph 3, no other royalties or payments of any kind shall be due from Publisher to Composer.

4. It is agreed that all sums payable hereunder to the parties named as Composer shall be divided among them as follows:

NAME	SHARE
_____	_____
_____	_____
_____	_____
_____	_____

5. Publisher agrees to render statements and make payments to Composer annually for the period ending December 31 of each year within ninety (90) days after such date, but no statement need be rendered or payment made with respect to any year in which less than the sum of Five Dollars ($5.00) shall be due to Composer.

6. (Delete inapplicable section)

If Publisher has not published the composition two years after the date of this agreement, then at the option of either party this agreement may be cancelled, in which event the composition shall be returned to Composer and Publisher shall be relieved of all duty, liability and responsibility hereunder. Such option may not be exercised by Composer unless he shall have requested Publisher in writing to publish the composition and the Publisher shall have failed to do so within ninety (90) days after receipt of such request.

Publisher shall have the right but not the obligation at any time to publish or have published the composition. Composer shall have the option to cancel this agreement at the expiration of   years from the date hereof unless within such period of   years (a) Publisher has published the composition, or (b) a commercial phonograph recording thereof has been issued, or (c) Publisher has produced and paid for rental materials for the performance of the composition, or (d) Publisher has paid to Composer at least the sum of   Dollars ($) under this agreement and/or any other agreement between the parties relating wholly or in part to the composition. Such option may be exercised by written notice to Publisher given at least ninety days prior to the expiration of such period of   years, and if it is exercised, the composition shall be returned to Composer and Publisher shall be relieved of all duty, liability and responsibility hereunder.

7. Composer agrees to secure and deliver to Publisher an assignment of copyright or other instrument of authorization relating to the text (if any) for the composition in the form and to the extent required by Publisher. Publisher shall have the right to expend such sums as may be necessary to obtain such instrument from the owner of the copyright in such text (if any), in which event all sums so expended by Publisher shall be for the account of Composer and shall be charged to Composer and may be deducted by Publisher from any moneys due to Composer under this or any other agreement between the parties.

8. Anything to the contrary notwithstanding, nothing in this agreement contained shall prevent Publisher from authorizing publishers, agents and representatives in countries outside of the United States and Canada (and in Canada if said composition is printed by a party other than Publisher in Canada) from exercising exclusive publication and all other rights in said foreign

countries in said composition, on the customary royalty basis; and nothing in this agreement shall prevent Publisher from authorizing publishers in the United States from exercising exclusive publication rights and other rights in the United States in said composition, provided Publisher shall pay Composer the royalties herein stipulated.

9. Composer may appoint a certified public accountant who shall, at any time during usual business hours, have access to all records of Publisher and of the United States publisher whom Publisher causes to publish said composition, relating to said composition, for the purpose of verifying royalty statements rendered, or which are delinquent under the terms hereof.

10. In the event that Publisher shall fail or refuse, within sixty days after written demand to furnish, or cause to be furnished, royalty statements described in paragraph 5, or to give Composer access to the records as set forth in paragraph 10, or in the event that Publisher shall fail to make payment of any royalty due, within thirty days after written demand therefor, then Composer shall have the option, to be exercised upon ten days' written notice, to cancel this agreement. Upon such cancellation, all rights of Publisher of any and every nature, in and to said composition, shall cease and come to an end and the said rights, including, but not limited to, the right to secure copyright and/or any copyright theretofore secured by Publisher, shall revert to, and become the property of, and shall be reassigned to Composer. Publisher agrees that it will thereupon execute any and all assignments or other documents which may be necessary or proper to vest the said rights in Composer.

11. Composer agrees that Publisher may make or have made any versions, arrangements, adaptations, interpolations, and translations of the composition, and the setting of words to music and of music to the words, and changes of the title, as Publisher may deem desirable.

12. If, after submission of a manuscript approved by Composer and after production has been commenced on the basis thereof, Composer suggests any alterations or revisions and such alterations or revisions are made by Publisher, the cost thereof shall be borne by Composer.

13. Composer consents to the use of Composer's name and likeness on and in connection with published copies and recordings of the composition, and in publicity, promotional material and advertising concerning the composition and Publisher.

14. Written demands and notices other than royalty statements provided for herein shall be sent by registered mail.

15. Any legal action brought by Publisher against any alleged infringer of said composition shall be initiated and prosecuted at its sole expense, and of any recovery made by it as a result thereof, after deduction of the expense of the litigation, a sum equal to fifty percent (50%) shall be paid to Composer.

(a) If a claim is presented against Publisher alleging that the said composition is an infringement upon some other composition, and because thereof Publisher is jeopardized, it shall thereupon serve written notice upon Composer containing the full details of such claim and thereafter, until the claim has been adjudicated or settled, shall withhold any moneys coming due Composer pending the outcome of such claim; provided, however, if no suit be filed in twelve months after written notice to Composer by Publisher of the adverse claim, the said moneys shall be released and paid to Composer. Such payment shall be without prejudice to the rights of Publisher in the event of a subsequent adverse adjudication.

(b) From and after the service of a summons in a suit for infringement filed against Publisher in respect of said composition, any and all payments hereunder thereafter coming due Composer shall be retained by Publisher until the suit has been finally adjudicated and then be disbursed accordingly, unless Composer shall elect to file an acceptable bond in the sum of such payments, in which event the sums due shall be paid to Composer.

16. Composer agrees to indemnify, save and hold harmless Publisher and its licensees, successors and assigns, from and against all claims, actions, proceedings, liabilities and costs, including attorneys' fees, which may be asserted against or incurred by any of them, arising out of or connected with any claim by a third party which is inconsistent with any of the warranties or representations made by Composer in this agreement or by reason of the exercise of any of

the rights granted or purported to be granted by this agreement. Composer authorizes Publisher in its sole discretion and at Composer's expense to employ attorneys and to defend any action or proceedings and/or to take any other steps proper to protect the right, title and interest of Publisher in the composition and, in that connection, to settle, or in any other manner dispose of, any claim, action or proceeding and to satisfy any judgment. Composer agrees to reimburse Publisher for any such expenses on demand and authorizes Publisher to withhold any and all sums which may be or become due to Composer under this or any other agreement between the parties until such claim, action or proceeding shall have been disposed of or the breach of any warranty hereunder repaired.

17. Any controversy or claim relating or arising out of this agreement, or the breach thereof, shall be settled by arbitration in New York City in accordance with the Rules of the American Arbitration Association, and judgment upon the award rendered by the Arbitrator may be entered in any Court having jurisdiction thereof.

18. This agreement is binding upon the parties hereto and their respective successors and assigns.

19. This agreement represents the entire understanding between the parties. It may not be changed orally. It shall be construed according to the laws of the State of New York.

IN WITNESS WHEREOF, the parties hereto have caused the agreement to be duly executed the day and year first above written.

Witness: PUBLISHER

_____ By _____

                                                      President

Witness: COMPOSER _____

_____ Address _____

Witness: COMPOSER _____

_____ Address _____

EXTRACTS FROM ASCAP CREDIT WEIGHTING FORMULA
RELATING TO CREDITS FOR SERIOUS WORKS

(D) SERIOUS WORKS FOUR MINUTES OR LONGER IN DURATION

Works which require four minutes or more for a single, complete rendition thereof, and which in their original form were composed for a choral, symphonic, or similar concert performance (including chamber music), shall receive credit on the following basis when performed for the respective designated periods of time:

MINUTES OF ACTUAL PERFORMANCE	THE OTHERWISE APPLICABLE CREDIT IS MULTIPLIED BY:
4:00 to 5:30	2
5:31 to 10:30	5
10:31 to 15:30	9
15:31 to 20:30	14
20:31 to 25:30	20
25:31 to 30:30	28
30:31 to 35:30	36
35:31 to 40:30	44
40:31 to 45:30	52
45:31 to 50:30	60
50:31 to 55:30	68
55:31 to 60:30	76
Each additional 5 minutes or part thereof	8

Performances on national radio network sustaining programs consisting of concerts by symphony orchestras which are presented as a genuine contribution to the culture of the nation shall be awarded credit equal to performances on a radio network of 50 stations.

(E) CONCERT AND SYMPHONY PERFORMANCES

The license fees which the Society receives from concert and symphony halls shall be multiplied by five in determining the credit to be awarded for performances of works in concert and symphony halls. For performances in concert and symphony halls, points shall be awarded as follows:

112

POINT AWARD MINUTES

	Up to 5	6 to 10	11 to 15	16 to 20	21 to 30	31 to 45	46 to 60
A) ENTERTAINMENT MUSIC—i.e.							
Light or Standard Instrumental and Choral Music ALL CATEGORIES	1	2	3	4	5	6	7
B) SERIOUS MUSIC IN THE ORIGINAL FORM							
a. Works for 1 or 2 instruments with or without voice	2	4	6	8	10	12	14
b. Works for 3 to 9 instruments with or without voice	3	6	9	12	15	20	25
c. Works for small orchestra with or without voice	4	9	18	24	30	40	50
d. Works for full orchestra with or without voice	8	18	36	48	60	80	100

For works in excess of 60 minutes, pro rata on the basis of the 60 minute points. The percentage of credit for arrangements of works in the Public Domain will be determined in accordance with Section (F).

(H) CONCERT AND SYMPHONY PERFORMANCES — ADDITIONAL CREDIT

In the case of any work which qualifies for credit under subdivision (B) of paragraph (E) above, and for which the Society holds the right to license such work from a writer member of the Society, or holds the right to license such work from the writer under Section I of the Order, such work shall receive for performances under paragraph (E) above, additional credit under this section. The additional credit shall be determined by multiplying the credit such work received under paragraph (E) above by twice the ratio of (i) the license fees which the Society received from concert and symphony halls in the survey year October 1, 1963 through September 30, 1964 to (ii) the license fees which the Society received from concert and symphony halls in the year of the performance. Such additional credit shall in no event be more than twice the credit awarded under paragraph (E) above. Distribution based on the additional credits awarded under this paragraph shall be in addition to the distribution based upon credits awarded under paragraph (E) above.

Appendix H2

EXAMPLES OF THE LIMITATION UNDER ASCAP WEIGHTING RULES OF ADDITIONAL CREDIT FOR PERFORMANCES IN CONCERT AND SYMPHONY HALLS*

1. Assumed license fees received from concert and symphony halls for performances of serious music 10/1/63-9/30/64	$100,000	$100,000	$100,000	$100,000
2. Assumed license fees received from concert and symphony halls for performances of serious music — year subsequent to 10/1/63-9/30/64	$100,000	$150,000	$200,000	$ 80,000
3. Ratio of license fees for 10/1/63-9/30/64 to fees for year subsequent to 10/1/63-9/30/64 (line 1 ÷ line 2)	1.0	⅔	½	1.25
4. Two times ratio set forth in line 3; the product not to exceed 2	2.0	1.33	1	2.0
5. Credit under Paragraph E for serious works (assuming a credit value of $1.00) (line 2 times 5)	500,000	750,000	1,000,000	400,000
6. Additional credit under Paragraph H (credit under Paragraph E times line 4)	1,000,000	1,000,000	1,000,000	800,000
7. Total credits	1,500,000	1,750,000	2,000,000	1,200,000

Thus, on the foregoing assumptions, if a member has a serious work for which he received 100 credits under paragraph E of the Weighting Formula for a performance in a symphony or concert hall in December 1963, that member also received an additional 200 credits for the same performance under paragraph H. If the work is performed again in a year in which the Society's receipts from symphony and concert halls rose to $200,000, the member would receive for that performance 200 credits under paragraph E and an additional 200 credits under paragraph H, assuming that there were the same number of points awarded for performances of serious works in symphony and concert halls in both years.

In a year in which the Society's receipts from symphony and concert halls for performances of serious music went down to $80,000, that member would receive 80 credits under paragraph E and an additional 160 credits under paragraph H, also assuming that the number of points awarded for performances in symphony and concert halls were the same in both years.

* From Report to Members by ASCAP President Stanley Adams dated August 23, 1965, p. 11.

Appendix I

EXTRACT FROM ASCAP WRITERS' DISTRIBUTION FORMULA RELATING TO SPECIAL AWARDS

Notwithstanding any of the foregoing provisions, in calculating the total distributable revenues to be placed in the four funds referred to in Sections I through IV above or distributed pursuant to Section VII below, there may first be deducted an amount not exceeding 5% of such revenues prior to such deduction, for the purpose of making special awards to writers whose works have a unique prestige value for which adequate compensation would not otherwise be received by such writers, and to writers whose works are performed substantially in media not surveyed by the Society. The distribution of such awards shall be determined by an independent panel appointed for that purpose by the writer members of the Board of Directors, and 30 days prior to payment pursuant to any such awards, the Society shall send to all of its writer members a list of all recipients of such awards and the amount awarded to each.

Appendix J

FORM OF AMERICAN COMPOSERS ALLIANCE
ASSIGNMENT OF PERFORMING RIGHTS
BY ITS MEMBERS

ASSIGNMENT made this_____day of_____, 19_____, by the undersigned Composer to AMERICAN COMPOSERS ALLIANCE, a membership association having its principal place of business in the City of New York, N.Y., herein called "ACA".

WITNESSETH: That the Composer in consideration of the acceptance by ACA of his application for membership and other valuable considerations the receipt of which is hereby acknowledged, hereby assigns to ACA:

(1) The entire and exclusive performing rights throughout the world in all musical works written or acquired by the Composer prior to or during the term of this assignment or of any extension hereof (except any works listed on the annexed sheet in which rights have heretofore been assigned), including all rights of public performance by means of radio and television broadcast, telephony, wired wireless, synchronization with motion pictures, concert, dance or other programs, phonograph or other recordings, and any other method of transmitting or reproducing sound; but this assignment shall not include the right to perform an entire musical play, ballet, opera or operetta, having a performing time in excess of thirty minutes.

For the term of this assignment ACA is vested with the full right to license or to grant to others exclusive or limited rights to license performance rights in said works and to rent or make available to others all scores and parts thereof.

(2) This assignment includes the option hereby granted to ACA to secure and enforce all common law and statutory copyrights in such musical works in any manner it may elect including suit in the name of the Composer, ACA or its nominee, or otherwise, for which purpose the Composer hereby appoints ACA his agent.

(3) The Composer will execute such further instruments as ACA may deem advisable to confirm the rights and options hereby assigned.

(4) This assignment shall remain in full force and effect for the period of any assignment-of-rights contracts which ACA may from time to time make, renew or replace, and for one year thereafter. Such assignment shall go into full legal effect as of the date of acceptance of this application for membership. Such assignment is subject to all applicable provisions of the Articles of Association of ACA, as amended from time to time.

IN WITNESS WHEREOF, the Composer for himself, his legal representatives and assigns, has signed and sealed these presents as of the day and year first above written.

Witness:

_____   _____
                                             Composer

Date_____

Appendix K

ASCAP SYMPHONY LICENSE

Memorandum of Agreement between AMERICAN SOCIETY OF COMPOSERS, AUTHORS AND PUBLISHERS (hereinafter styled "Society") and

(hereinafter styled "Licensee"), as follows:

1. Society grants and Licensee accepts for a period of   commencing a license to publicly perform at

and at other auditoriums in which Licensee shall give performances while on tour, and not elsewhere, non-dramatic renditions of the separate musical compositions including symphonic and other concert works heretofore copyrighted or composed by members of Society and now or hereafter during the term hereof in the repertory of Society, or hereafter during the term hereof copyrighted or composed by members of Society, or of which Society shall have the right to license such performing rights.

2. This license is not assignable nor transferable by operation of law, devolution or otherwise, and is limited strictly to the Licensee and to the premises referred to in Paragraph "1" of this agreement. The license fee herein provided to be paid is based upon the performance of such non-dramatic renditions for the entertainment solely of such persons as may be physically present on or in the premises described, and does not authorize the broadcasting, or transmission by wire or otherwise, of such performances or renditions to persons outside of such premises, and no license is hereby granted for any such broadcasting or transmission.

3. This license shall not extend to or be deemed to include:

(a) Operatic or dramatico-musical works (including plays with music, revues and ballets) as such, in whole or in part, or songs or other excerpts from operas or musical plays accompanied either by pantomime, dance or visual representation of the work from which the music is taken; but fragments or instrumental selections from such works may be instrumentally rendered without dialogue, costume, accompanying dramatic action or scenic accessory, and unaccompanied by any stage action or visual representation of the work of which such music forms a part.

(b) The right to perform any special orchestral arrangements or transcriptions of the musical compositions licensed hereunder unless such arrangements or transcriptions have been copyrighted by members of Society or by members of foreign societies which have granted to Society the right to license such performances.

4. Society reserves the right at any time to restrict the first American performance of any composition in its repertory and further reserves the right at any time to withdraw from its repertory and from operation of this license, any musical work as to which any suit has been brought or threatened on a claim that such composition infringes a composition not contained in Society's repertory, or on a claim that Society does not have the right to license the performing rights in such composition.

5. (a) Society agrees to indemnify, save and hold Licensee and its artists and the proprietors of the premises mentioned in Paragraph "1" harmless, and defend Licensee and its artists and the proprietors of said premises from and against any claim, demand or suit that may be made or brought against them or any of them with respect to renditions given by Licensee during the term hereof in accordance with this license of "cleared compositions," or of musical compositions heretofore copyrighted or composed by members of Society and now or hereafter during the term hereof in Society's repertory, or hereafter during the term hereof copyrighted or composed by present members of Society or by future members of Society so long as such future members shall be members of Society. In the event of the service upon Licensee of any notice, process, paper or pleading under which a claim, demand or action is made or begun against Licensee on account of any such matter as is hereinabove referred to, Licensee shall promptly give Society written notice thereof and simultaneously therewith deliver to Society any such notice, process, paper or pleading, or a copy thereof, and Society at its own expense shall have sole charge of the defense of any such action or proceeding. Licensee, however, shall have the right to engage counsel of its own, at its own expense, who may participate in the defense of any such action or proceeding and with whom counsel for Society shall cooperate. Licensee shall cooperate with Society in every way in the defense of any such action or proceeding, and in any appeals that may be taken from any judgments or orders entered therein, and shall execute all pleadings, bonds or other instruments, but at the sole expense of Society, that may be required in order properly to defend and resist any such action or proceeding, and prosecute any appeals taken therein. In the event of the service upon Licensee of any notice, process, paper or pleading under which a claim, demand or action is made, or begun against Licensee on account of the rendition by Licensee of any musical composition (other than a "cleared composition") contained in Society's repertory but not heretofore or hereafter during the term hereof copyrighted or composed by members of Society, Society agrees at the request of Licensee to cooperate with and assist Licensee in the defense of any such action or proceeding, and in any appeals that Licensee may elect to take from any judgments or orders entered therein.

(b) As used in this Paragraph "5" a "cleared composition" shall mean any composition which Society shall have notified Licensee is a composition with respect to which Society is willing to indemnify Licensee, provided that the Society may limit such indemnity to a specific program of Licensee for which a clearance shall have been given by Society.

6. Licensee agrees to furnish to Society each week a program containing a list of all musical compositions performed by Licensee in each of its performances during the previous week at said premises as well as on tour, including all encores.

7. Upon any breach or default of any term or condition herein contained by either party, the other party may give the party in default thirty (30) days' notice in writing to cure such breach or default, and in the event that such breach or default has not been cured within said thirty (30) days, the party giving such notice may then promptly terminate this license.

8. The parties hereto hereby agree that this agreement shall be deemed to be, and the same shall be, extended and renewed from year to year, unless either party, on or before thirty days next preceding the termination of any year, shall give notice in writing to the other by registered United States mail of the desire to terminate the same at the conclusion of such year.

9. Licensee agrees to pay Society for the license herein the sum of   Dollars
($) annually, payable

IN WITNESS WHEREOF, this agreement has been duly subscribed and sealed by Society and Licensee

this   day of   19

AMERICAN SOCIETY OF COMPOSERS,
AUTHORS AND PUBLISHERS

By..

....
LICENSEE

By..

Appendix L

ASCAP COLLEGES AND UNIVERSITIES LICENSE

AGREEMENT between American Society of Composers, Authors and Publishers ("Society") and

("University"), as follows:

1. Society grants and University accepts for a period of one year commencing

, a non-exclusive license to publicly perform in concerts, recitals, festivals, entertainments and all other similar events presented under the sole auspices of University, at its university premises (including other premises in the United States engaged by University exclusively), and not elsewhere, non-dramatic renditions of the separate musical compositions of which Society shall, during the term hereof, have the right to license such performing rights. This license does not extend to or include the public performance or any rendition or performance of any opera, operetta, musical comedy, play or like production as such, in whole or in part.

2. This license is not assignable nor transferable by operation of law, devolution or otherwise, and is limited strictly to the University and to the premises referred to in Paragraph "1" of this agreement. The license fee herein provided to be paid is based upon the performance of such non-dramatic renditions for the entertainment solely of such persons as may be physically present on or in the premises described, and does not authorize the broadcasting, telecasting, or transmission by wire or otherwise of such performances or renditions, and no license is hereby granted for any such broadcasting, telecasting, or transmission.

3. This license shall not extend to or be deemed to include or authorize (a) the recording of, or the manufacture of, any recordings, or any other device used as a means of reproducing any musical composition of which the right of performance is licensed under this agreement; or (b) the copying or other reproduction, in whole or in part, by any means, method or process whatsoever, of any vocal or instrumental score or part of any musical composition of which the right of performance is licensed under this agreement; or (c) the performance of any special orchestral arrangements or transcriptions of the musical compositions licensed hereunder unless such arrangements or transcriptions have been copyrighted by members of Society or by members of foreign societies which have granted to Society the right to license such performances.

4. Society reserves the right at any time to withdraw from its repertory and from the operation of this license, any musical work as to which any suit has been brought or threatened on a claim that such composition infringes a composition not contained in Society's repertory, or on a claim that Society does not have the right to license the performing rights in such composition.

5. University agrees to furnish to Society a schedule of all musical events to be presented by University during the term of this agreement. In addition, University agrees to furnish to Society each month during the term hereof a program or programs containing a list of all musical compositions, including all encores, performed by University in each of its concerts, recitals, festivals, entertainments and other similar events during the previous month at the premises described in Paragraph "1" of this agreement. It is agreed that if information is not readily available in this form, the furnishing by University to Society of copies of programs of musical performances which are prepared for distribution to the audience, or for the use or information of the University or any department thereof, shall constitute full performance by University under this Paragraph "5".

6. In consideration of the license herein granted, UNIVERSITY agrees to pay to SOCIETY the following sum based on UNIVERSITY's total student enrollment:

    A. $25.00 if such enrollment is less than 1,000;

    B. $75.00 if such enrollment is between 1,000 and 5,000;

    C. $125.00 if such enrollment is between 5,001 and 10,000;

    D. $200.00 if such enrollment is over 10,000.

7. The payment specified in Paragraph "6" shall be made within thirty (30) days after the execution of this agreement and shall be accompanied by a certified statement on a form to be supplied by SOCIETY, showing UNIVERSITY's total student enrollment. In the event that this agreement shall be extended as provided in Paragraph "9", the fee for each succeeding year shall be paid within thirty (30) days after such extension shall become effective, and each payment shall be accompanied by a form to be supplied by SOCIETY showing the total student enrollment for each succeeding year.

8. Upon any breach or default by UNIVERSITY of any terms herein contained, SOCIETY may give UNIVERSITY thirty (30) days' notice in writing to cure such breach or default, and in the event such breach or default has not been cured within the said thirty (30) days, SOCIETY may then forthwith terminate this license.

9. This agreement shall be extended from year to year, unless either party shall give notice in writing to the other, not less than thirty (30) days prior to the termination of this agreement (or any extension thereof) of its desire to terminate the same at the conclusion of such year.

10. All notices required or permitted to be given by either of the parties to the other hereunder shall be duly and properly given if mailed to such other party by registered or certified United States mail, addressed to such other party at its main office for the transaction of business.

IN WITNESS WHEREOF this agreement has been duly executed by SOCIETY and UNIVERSITY, this

day of   , 19   .

AMERICAN SOCIETY OF COMPOSERS,
AUTHORS AND PUBLISHERS

By ....

....

By ....

Appendix M

SECTION 104 OF COPYRIGHT LAW OF THE UNITED STATES OF AMERICA
(United States Code, Title 17 — Copyrights)*

WILLFUL INFRINGEMENT FOR PROFIT. — Any person who willfully and for profit shall infringe any copyright secured by this title, or who shall knowingly and willfully aid or abet such infringement, shall be deemed guilty of a misdemeanor, and upon conviction thereof shall be punished by imprisonment for not exceeding one year or by a fine of not less than $100 nor more than $1000, or both, in the discretion of the court: *Provided, however*, that nothing in this title shall be so construed as to prevent the performance of religious or secular works such as oratorios, cantatas, masses, or octavo choruses by public schools, church choirs, or vocal societies, rented, borrowed, or obtained from some public library, public school, church choir, school choir, or vocal society, provided the performance is given for charitable or educational purposes and not for profit.

* Act of July 30, 1947 (61 Stat. 652), as amended.

Appendix N

FORM OF LICENSE AGREEMENT FOR FOLIOS

Date:

Music Publisher
Brill Building
New York, N.Y.

Gentlemen:

The following is the agreement between you and us.

1. You hereby grant to us the exclusive right and license during the term hereof to print, publish and sell, at our own cost and expense, your copyrighted musical composition (herein called "composition") entitled:_____, and written by:_____in any and all editions thereof as we may elect, other than piano-vocal (regular sheet music), in the United States, its territories and possessions, and the Dominion of Canada, at such prices and on terms and discounts as we in our sole discretion may determine from time to time.

2. As and for compensation for said right and license, we shall pay you royalties on ninety (90%) per cent of any and all copies of the composition which we, during the term hereof, authorize to be printed, irrespective of whether or when the same may be sold. The said royalties, to be calculated on print orders, shall be computed at the following rates:

(A) Ten (10%) per cent of the retail selling price of each copy so printed by us in a dance orchestration, stage dance band, concert or marching band, or choral edition, and

(B) Twenty (20%) per cent of the retail selling price of each copy so printed by us as an accordion, guitar, organ or other instrumental solo, and

(C) A pro-rata share of ten (10%) per cent of the retail selling price of each folio, book or other collection so printed by us in which the lyrics and/or music of the composition shall be included by us, based on the total number of copyrighted works contained in each collective publication.

3. We shall account to you on a monthly basis for all royalties payable to you and shall simultaneously pay you all sums due to you. Each accounting shall set forth in detail the computation of the payments due and shall include, without limitation of the generality of the foregoing, the types of editions, the number of copies printed and the royalty rates applied. You agree that our accountings to you hereunder shall be deemed conclusive and binding upon you unless, within one year from the date of each accounting, we shall receive written notice from you specifying all disputes, errors and omissions asserted by you. You shall have the right to examine our books and records and those of our affiliates during reasonable hours, on ten (10) days written notice, regarding all matters hereunder.

4. For the purpose of computation of royalties, each edition shall not consist of more than twenty-five (25) songs without your consent.

5. Each copy of the composition as published by us shall bear your name as the copyright owner, with the form of copyright notice prescribed by you.

6. The title of the composition shall not be in the main title of the folio without your consent.

122

7. You warrant and represent that you are the sole owner of the composition and the copyrights thereon for the licensed territory, that you have the sole right and authority to enter into this agreement, and that the composition is original and does not infringe upon the rights of third parties. You agree to indemnify and save us harmless of and from any and all liabilities, damages, costs and expenses, including reasonable attorneys' fees, suffered or incurred by us by reason of a breach or claim of breach of your covenants and warranties hereunder. We agree to give you immediate written notice of any adverse claim and to permit you to defend in our behalf by a counsel chosen by you.

8. If we fail to account and make payments hereunder and such failure is not cured within ten (10) days after written notice thereof is sent to us by registered mail, or if we fail to perform any other obligations required of us hereunder and such failure is not cured within thirty (30) days after written notice to us by registered mail, or in the event we go into compulsory liquidation or bankruptcy or make an assignment for the benefit of creditors or make any compositions with creditors, or any insolvency or composition proceeding shall be commenced by or against us, then and in any of such events you, in addition to such other rights and remedies which you may have at law or otherwise under this agreement, may elect to cancel or terminate this agreement without prejudice to any rights or claims you may have, and all rights hereunder shall forthwith revert to you and we may not thereafter exercise any rights hereunder and shall destroy all printed copies in our possession. Your failure to terminate this agreement upon any default or defaults shall not be deemed to constitute a waiver of your right to terminate the same upon any subsequent default.

9. This agreement and our rights hereunder shall be in full force and effect for a period of one (1) year from the date hereof and shall continue in effect thereafter until terminated by you or us by a ninety (90) day prior written notice by registered mail which may become effective at the close of such year or thereafter. You agree that notwithstanding such termination by you, for a period of one (1) year after termination, we shall continue to have the right to market and sell any and all copies of the composition then on hand, provided and on condition that within thirty (30) days following the termination date we supply you with a written inventory of the number of copies of each edition then on hand.

10. This agreement shall not be construed as one of partnership or joint venture.

11. This agreement shall be construed and interpreted under the laws of the State of New York applicable to agreements wholly to be performed therein.

Please indicate your acceptance of the foregoing by signing at the place indicated below.

Very truly yours,

FOLIO PUBLISHER

BY_____

AGREED TO AND ACCEPTED:

MUSIC PUBLISHER

BY_____

Appendix O

FORM OF LICENSE AGREEMENT FOR SHEET MUSIC

Date:

Music Publisher
Brill Building
New York, N.Y.

Gentlemen:

The following is the agreement between you and us:

1. You hereby appoint us your sole and exclusive selling agent and distributor of all piano/vocal editions of your said composition in the United States of America, its territories and possessions, and the Dominion of Canada.

2. We agree, at our own cost and expense, to undertake for such territory the entire project of printing and offering for sale all regular piano/vocal copies of your musical composition entitled:

and written by:

By this commitment, we agree to pay all preparation and production expenses for such piano/vocal editions, including art work, arranging and printing costs. The list price shall be seventy-five (75¢) cents per copy and we shall initially offer same for sale on a fully returnable basis.

3. We agree to account and pay to you a sum representing twenty-five (25¢) cents per copy on all sales of piano/vocal copies, for which we shall have received payment, as follows:

(A) Ninety (90) days after we shall notify all of our customers that return privileges are no longer applicable to the composition, we shall account and pay to you on all paid sales made on our fully returnable terms, and

(B) Thereafter we shall account and pay to you on a quarter-annual basis on all paid sales thereof made on our non-returnable terms.

(C) During the period within which said composition shall be offered for sale by us on a fully returnable basis, we shall furnish you with monthly progress reports thereon.

(D) Our accountings pursuant to subdivision (B) above shall be rendered to you within forty-five (45) days after the close of each such accounting period and shall be conclusive and binding upon you unless we shall receive written notice from you, specifying all disputes, errors, and omissions asserted by you, within one (1) year from the date of each such respective accounting.

4. You shall have the right by representatives chosen by you to examine during ordinary business hours all books and records maintained by us or our affiliates and relating to matters hereunder.

5. Each copy of said composition printed hereunder shall bear your name as the copyright proprietor, with a copyright notice prescribed by you. When we print copies we shall place copies on sale in Canada prior to or simultaneously with the inception of sales in the United States of America and shall secure in your name a Certificate of Sale for the composition. We shall deliver such certificate to you together with 25 copies of the composition, and you shall be responsible for securing your registration of copyright thereof in the United States of America.

6. You warrant and represent that you are the sole and absolute owner of the composition and the copyrights thereon for said territory, that you have the sole and exclusive right and authority to enter into this agreement and that the composition is original and does not infringe upon the rights of third parties. You agree to indemnify and save us harmless of and from any and all liabilities, damages, costs and expenses, including reasonable attorneys' fees, suffered or incurred by us by reason of a breach or claim of breach of your covenants and warranties hereunder. We agree to give you immediate written notice of any adverse claim and to permit you to defend in our behalf by a counsel chosen by you.

7. If we fail to account and make payments hereunder and such failure is not cured within ten (10) days after written notice thereof is sent to us by registered mail, or if we fail to perform any other obligations required of us hereunder and such failure is not cured within thirty (30) days after written notice to us by registered mail, or in the event we go into compulsory liquidation or bankruptcy or make an assignment for the benefit of creditors or make any compositions with creditors, or any insolvency or composition proceeding shall be commenced by or against us, then and in any of such events you, in addition to such other rights and remedies which you may have at law or otherwise under this agreement, may elect to cancel or terminate this agreement without prejudice to any rights or claims you may have, and all rights hereunder shall forthwith revert to you and we may not thereafter exercise any rights hereunder and shall destroy all printed copies in our possession. Your failure to terminate this agreement upon any default or defaults shall not be deemed to constitute a waiver of your right to terminate the same upon any subsequent default.

8. This agreement and our rights hereunder shall be in full force and effect for a period of one (1) year from the date hereof and shall automatically continue to be effective after said stated term unless terminated by either party at the end of such period or subsequently on ninety (90) days prior written notice sent by registered mail. You agree that notwithstanding such termination by you we shall have the right to market, sell and authorize the continued sale of any and all copies of said composition then on hand, for a period of a year after termination.

9. This agreement may be assigned by us in whole or in part to any of our affiliated subsidiary companies provided that we remain liable for performance hereunder, but may not otherwise be assigned by either you or us without the other's express written consent.

10. This agreement shall not be construed as one of partnership or joint venture.

11. This agreement shall be construed and interpreted under the laws of the State of New York applicable to agreements wholly to be performed therein.

Please signify your acceptance of the foregoing by signing at the place indicated below.

Very truly yours,

SHEET MUSIC LICENSEE

BY_____

AGREED TO AND ACCEPTED:

MUSIC PUBLISHER

BY_____

Appendix P

FORM OF SELLING AGENCY AGREEMENT FOR SHEET MUSIC
(Invoices Issued in Name of Agent)

Date:

Music Publisher
Brill Building
New York, N.Y.

Gentlemen:

The following is the agreement between you and us:

1. You hereby appoint us and we agree to act as your sole and exclusive selling agent and distributor in the United States of America, its territories and possessions, and the Dominion of Canada, on the terms and conditions herein set forth, for regular piano-vocal copies of your musical composition entitled:

and written by:

(hereinafter referred to as "the composition").

2. If you do not furnish us with sufficient printed copies of the composition for resale, then, until you shall give us written directions to the contrary, you agree that we shall, at your sole cost and expense, cause the composition to be printed. We shall furnish you with the original copies of bills rendered to us in connection with the said printing, and shall advise you of printing costs and the place of printing in advance of giving orders for such printing. In the event your printing is serviced through us, you agree to pay us and hereby authorize us to charge your account with the sum of Fifteen ($15) Dollars for the use of our production facilities, which charge shall be made only at the time of the initial printing of the composition and shall not be applicable to reprints.

You agree to pay to us the sum of_____as an advance against our production costs hereunder with respect to the composition.

3. You agree that all copies of said composition shall be sold and distributed through us at such list prices and on such terms and conditions as we may in our sole discretion establish from time to time in the exercise of good faith, including but not limited to special "rack" jobber and other discounts. You acknowledge that until we determine to market said composition as a standard non-returnable publication, the composition shall be sold by us with full return privileges.

4. So long as we shall have any transactions with respect to the composition, we agree to render regular monthly statements to you showing the number of copies sold and paid for, the number of copies returned, and indicating the debits and credits in your general account with us. Subject to the deduction of our commissions and of printing and other costs chargeable to you, and subject to our establishing a reasonable reserve against contingent returns, we shall simultaneously remit to you the balance of the net moneys actually received by us from the paid sales of the composition. Thirty (30) days after the date that return privileges are no longer applicable to the composition, we shall make final settlement with you with respect to returnable sales.

With respect to sales on non-returnable terms, we shall render regular monthly statements together with payments due you in regard to all such sales.

5. As compensation for our services hereunder, you agree to pay us commissions in a sum equal to the following percentages of the gross wholesale selling price to jobbers on all paid sales of the composition:

Fifteen (15%) per cent on the returnable edition; and
Twenty (20%) per cent on the non-returnable edition.

You hereby irrevocably authorize and empower us to retain and deduct our said commissions in our accountings with you.

6. You shall have the right, by representatives of your own choosing, to examine during ordinary business hours all of our books and records and those of our affiliates relating to matters hereunder.

7. We agree that all copies of the composition which we cause to be printed shall bear your name as the copyright proprietor, with a copyright notice prescribed by you. We also agree to place copies of the composition on sale in Canada prior to or simultaneously with the inception of sales in the United States of America, to secure a Certificate of Sale for the composition and to deliver the Certificate to you together with 25 copies of the composition. You shall be responsible for securing your registration of the copyright thereof in the United States of America.

8. You hereby agree that all copies of the composition which may be printed during the term hereof shall be prominently imprinted with the following notice:

Sole Selling Agent: Independent Distributor
106 Carmody Street
New York 1, N.Y.

9. We agree to use our best efforts in the marketing and promotion of the printed edition of the composition through circulars, trade lists and other customary modes of promotion, so as to acquaint the entire trade with its availability. No charge shall be made to you for promotion.

10. You warrant that you are the sole owner of the composition and the copyrights thereon for the licensed territory, that you have the sole right and authority to enter into this agreement and that the composition is original and does not infringe upon the rights of third parties. You agree to indemnify and save us harmless from liabilities, damages, costs and expenses, including reasonable counsel fees, suffered or incurred by us by reason of a breach or claim of breach of your covenants and warranties hereunder. We agree to give you immediate written notice of any adverse claim and to permit you to defend on our behalf by a counsel chosen by you.

11. If we fail to account and make payments hereunder and such failure is not cured within ten (10) days after written notice thereof is sent to us by registered mail, or if we fail to perform any other obligations required of us hereunder and such failure is not cured within thirty (30) days after written notice to us by registered mail, or in the event we go into compulsory liquidation or bankruptcy or make an assignment for the benefit of creditors or make any compositions with creditors, or any insolvency or composition proceeding shall be commenced by or against us, then and in any of such events you, in addition to such other rights and remedies which you may have at law or otherwise under this agreement, may elect to cancel or terminate this agreement without prejudice to any rights or claims you may have, and all rights hereunder shall forthwith revert to you and we may not thereafter exercise any rights hereunder and shall thereupon return the inventory of your printed editions to you. Your failure to terminate this agreement upon any default or defaults shall not be deemed to constitute a waiver of your right to terminate the same upon any subsequent default.

12. This agreement shall continue for a term of one (1) year from date and shall continue thereafter unless and until terminated at the end of such one (1) year period or subsequently by a written notice of termination given by either party by registered mail at least sixty (60) days prior to the termination date. At or before the termination date we shall return the inventory of your printed editions to you, together with statements as at such date. If our present management or ownership is changed, you may terminate this agreement at any time thereafter upon sixty (60) days written notice by registered mail.

13. This agreement shall not be construed as one of partnership or joint venture.

14. This agreement shall be construed and interpreted under the laws of the State of New York applicable to agreements wholly to be performed therein.

Please signify your acceptance of the foregoing by signing at the place indicated below.

Very truly yours,

INDEPENDENT DISTRIBUTOR

BY_____

AGREED TO AND ACCEPTED:

MUSIC PUBLISHER

BY_____

Appendix Q

FORM OF CATALOG SELLING AGENCY AGREEMENT FOR ALL PRINTED EDITIONS
(Invoices Issued in Name of Principal)

Date:

Music Publisher
Brill Building
New York City, New York

Gentlemen:

The following is the agreement between you and us:

1. You hereby appoint us, and we agree to act as, the sole and exclusive selling agent and distributor for printed editions in your catalog, for the territory of the United States, its territories and possessions, and the Dominion of Canada.

2. For the purpose of this agreement, your catalog shall consist of any and all printed editions, containing your musical compositions, that you may own or otherwise control during the term hereof.

3. You agree to furnish us with copies of the printed editions in your catalog for our sale and distribution. You will pay directly all expenses involved in the production of the printed editions, including engraving, autographing, artwork, type and printing. We agree to cooperate with you in connection with such production, including the making available of our production facilities.

4. We agree to maintain a separate set of accounts receivable books for your firm. Such books and records will contain complete information covering all transactions in connection with the sale and distribution of your printed editions. You hereby authorize us to have printed, at your cost, the necessary invoices bearing the name of your firm and our address.

5. We shall send to you monthly statements showing the number sold of each type of printed edition, together with checks received by us for sales of your printed editions. You agree to pay us, after the tenth of each month, the amount due us as compensation, in accordance with the provisions of Paragraph 7 hereof, for printed editions sold and paid for through the end of the previous month. We shall also render to you a monthly statement for money expended for postage, and you will issue a separate certified check made payable to "Postmaster" for the amount due, to be sent to us with the payment of our compensation. You shall have the right, by representatives of your own choosing, to examine during ordinary business hours all of our books and records and those of our affiliates relating to matters hereunder.

6. We agree to use our best efforts in the marketing and promotion of your printed editions through circulars, trade lists and other customary modes of promotion, so as to acquaint the entire trade with their availability. No charge shall be made to you for promotion.

7. In full consideration for our services and expenses other than postage, you agree to pay us as follows:

Fifteen (15%) per cent of all moneys received from the sale of printed editions in your catalog.

8. You warrant that you are the sole owner of the printed editions which are the subject of this agreement, that you have the sole right and authority to enter into this agreement with respect to such printed editions, and that the printed editions will not infringe upon the rights of third parties. You agree to indemnify and save us harmless of and from any and all liabilities, damages, costs and expenses, including reasonable counsel fees, suffered or incurred by us by reason of a breach or claim of breach of your covenants and warranties hereunder. We agree to give you immediate written notice of any adverse claim and to permit you to defend on our behalf by a counsel chosen by you.

9. Each copy of your printed editions printed under our control shall bear your name as the copyright proprietor with a notice prescribed by you. We agree to place copies of each such edition on sale in Canada prior to or simultaneously with the inception of sales in the United States of America, to secure a Certificate of Sale for the printed edition and to deliver the Certificate to you together with 25 copies of the printed edition. You shall be responsible for securing your registration of the copyright thereof in the United States of America.

10. If we fail to account and make payments hereunder and such failure is not cured within ten (10) days after written notice thereof is sent to us by registered mail, or if we fail to perform any other obligations required of us hereunder and such failure is not cured within thirty (30) days after written notice to us by registered mail, or in the event we go into compulsory liquidation or bankruptcy or make an assignment for the benefit of creditors or make any compositions with creditors, or any insolvency or composition proceeding shall be commenced by or against us, then and in any of such events you, in addition to such other rights and remedies which you may have at law or otherwise under this agreement, may elect to cancel or terminate this agreement without prejudice to any rights or claims you may have, and all rights hereunder shall forthwith revert to you and we may not thereafter exercise any rights hereunder and shall thereupon return the inventory of your printed editions to you. Your failure to terminate this agreement upon any default or defaults shall not be deemed to constitute a waiver of your right to terminate the same upon any subsequent default.

11. This agreement shall be for a period of two (2) years and shall continue thereafter unless and until terminated at the end of such two (2) year period or subsequently by a written notice of termination given by either party by registered mail at least sixty (60) days prior to the termination date. At or before the termination date we shall return the inventory of your printed editions to you, together with statements as at such date. If our present management or ownership is changed, you may terminate this agreement at any time thereafter upon sixty (60) days written notice.

12. This agreement shall not be construed as one of partnership or joint venture.

13. This agreement shall be construed and interpreted under the laws of the State of New York applicable to agreements wholly to be performed therein.

Please signify your acceptance of the foregoing by signing at the place indicated below.

Very truly yours,

SELLING AGENT

BY_____

AGREED TO AND ACCEPTED:

MUSIC PUBLISHER

BY_____

Appendix R

FORM OF LICENSE AGREEMENT FOR
SONG LYRIC REPRINT RIGHTS

Date:

Song Lyric Magazine
Tenth Avenue
Nashville, Tennessee

Gentlemen:
    The following is our agreement:

    1. We hereby grant to you and your affiliates the non-exclusive license to print and vend in song lyric publications in the United States, its territories and possessions, and the Dominion of Canada, the lyrics for the following musical composition(s) for a period of one (1) year from the date hereof:

    2. You agree to pay us for the rights herein granted, provided the lyrics of said musical composition(s) are available to you during the period of this agreement, the sum of_____ _____Dollars per song, receipt of which is hereby acknowledged.

    3. In the event that during the period of this agreement said musical composition(s) is (are) included among the top ten most popular songs in the country on the Billboard Hot 100 Chart of Hits, you shall pay us the additional sum of_____Dollars per song, on such Chart, provided said lyrics are available to you at such time.

    4. We warrant and represent that the lyrics furnished to you are new and original, that they do not infringe upon the rights of third parties and that we have the sole right and authority to enter into this agreement. We agree to indemnify and save you harmless of and from any and all liabilities, damages, costs and expenses, including reasonable counsel fees, suffered or incurred by you by reason of a breach or claim of breach of our covenants and warranties hereunder. You agree to give us immediate written notice of any adverse claim and to permit us to defend on your behalf by a counsel chosen by us.

    5. You agree that all copies of the lyrics of our composition(s) printed hereunder shall carry an appropriate copyright notice, furnished by us, showing our ownership of the copyright of the said composition(s).

    6. This agreement shall be binding on the parties hereto and their successors and assigns. You agree to remain liable at all times for performance of your covenants hereunder.

Very truly yours,

MUSIC PUBLISHER

BY_____

AGREED TO AND ACCEPTED:

SONG LYRIC MAGAZINE

BY_____

Appendix S

FORM OF BACKGROUND MUSIC TRANSCRIPTION LICENSE BY PUBLISHER
(Used by Harry Fox Office)

Gentlemen:

Upon my receipt of two copies hereof, signed by you below under the wording "Consented And Agreed To," this will constitute our agreement as follows:

I hereby grant you a license for the term hereof, being for the period of three years from January 1, 1963, to record and reproduce copies of such recordings of the copyrighted musical compositions of the music publishers whom I represent as Agent and Trustee which are available for such purpose, a list of such publishers being annexed hereto as "Exhibit A" and made a part hereof, for the limited purpose of making the same available for public performance for profit, in places where musical compositions are performed in the United States, such rights being confined to making the same available only for the limited purpose under the purview of that part of Section 1(e) of the Copyright Act preceding the mechanical reproduction proviso thereof, subject to the terms and conditions hereinafter set forth.

1. The rights granted hereunder with respect to each such composition shall comprehend the following:

(a) The right to make an arrangement, adaptation and transposition to adapt the same for the purpose of such recording thereof, provided, however, that no arrangement, adaptation or transposition made by you shall modify the fundamental character of the composition, and provided further that such arrangement, adaptation or transposition shall not be printed or used for any other purpose.

(b) The right to record in whole or in part, with or without the lyrics thereof, and in connection with other musical compositions or in connection with any words, phrases, dialogue or other material, except that no right is granted to change the lyrics of songs or substitute new lyrics therefor, or to record lyrics in connection with musical compositions that are not songs.

(c) The right to make, use and dispose of copies of such recordings for the limited purposes specifically set forth in paragraph "2" hereof.

(d) The right to make or manufacture shall be deemed to include and extend to the right to import the same into the United States and any such importation shall be considered a manufacture.

2. This license is merely one permitting the recording and reproduction of a certain type of copies of the recording of a musical composition such as an electrical transcription, in the form now known or any substitute therefor or replacement thereof now known or hereafter created and nothing herein contained shall be construed as a license, authority or permission for "broadcasting," as hereinafter defined, or any other public performance for profit of the musical compositions of my principals or recordings or copies thereof produced pursuant hereto.

The wording "available for public performance for profit" as used in the preamble hereof shall be deemed to include radio stations engaged in "broadcasting," as hereinafter defined, and other places where public performances are given such as restaurants, cabarets, factories, educational institutions, department stores, trains and other similar establishments, but no public performance for profit of any of the musical compositions, or of reproductions or copies of the recordings thereof made pursuant hereto, shall be made or caused to be made unless the place where such performance is given shall have a valid license to perform the same from the copyright proprietor thereof or the person, firm, association or corporation duly empowered to act on behalf of such copyright proprietor.

The word "broadcasting" shall be deemed to comprehend broadcasting by either so-called space radio (including by AM, FM and broadcasting in connection with television) or so-called wired radio, and the words "radio station" shall be deemed to comprehend stations broadcasting by AM, FM or broadcasting in connection with television.

It is specifically agreed that all dramatic and so-called "grand rights" are expressly excluded from this license and that you shall have no right whatsoever to make any such use of any musical composition nor to make any reproduction or copy thereof in such a way as will constitute such reproduction a dramatic use.

3. In consideration of the license hereby granted, you agree to make the following payments to me:

(a) On all of your recordings, you will pay me the sum of $12.50 per recording for said three year period. On each of your recordings released after January 1, 1966, you will pay me 1/36 of $12.50 for each month that each such recording is released prior to December 31, 1968. Upon payment therefor, all such recordings shall be licensed for the balance of the three year term.

(b) It is understood that a royalty of less than $12.50 for said three year period for each musical composition shall be mutually agreed upon with respect to recordings of medleys made of the musical compositions of the same publisher and by the same author or authors and it is further understood that with respect to any such medleys consisting of not more than four musical compositions, the fee will be $25.00 for the said three year period.

Any recordings and reproductions of copies of copyrighted musical compositions of my principals that you have made in conformity with the provisions of this license, and with respect to which you have made the foregoing payments, shall be deemed to have been lawfully made and may be used by you in the conduct of your business subject to all of the terms and conditions herein specified.

It is understood that the recordings and reproductions of copies thus made when used in connection with "broadcasting" as defined in paragraph "2" hereof, on locally sponsored broadcasts or on nationally sponsored broadcasts as defined in paragraph "4" hereof, shall be subject to the terms and conditions hereof.

4. For the purposes of this agreement a locally sponsored broadcast shall be deemed to mean a program advertising a business or service that is purely local in character, solely confined within the area of the station's coverage and broadcast over the station's facilities only, but shall be deemed to include a program that is purely local in character, solely confined within the area of the station's coverage that is broadcast over the station's facilities only, even though it is paid for in part, but not in whole, by a national advertiser, provided that such program is not one, the musical content of which was selected by a national advertiser, and is not a program which was prepared by a national advertiser for national or regional dissemination. All other sponsored broadcasts shall be deemed to be nationally sponsored broadcasts. The use of such recordings in restaurants, cabarets, factories, educational institutions, department stores, trains and other similar establishments shall be deemed to be in the same category as the use thereof in connection with a locally sponsored broadcast.

5. In the event that any recordings and reproductions of copies made pursuant to this license are used on nationally sponsored broadcasts, you agree to make a separate copy for each station using the same for such nationally sponsored broadcast and to collect and pay for each such copy manufactured by you and used in such broadcasts the sum of twenty-five (25¢) cents for each copyrighted musical composition licensed hereunder and embodied therein when such composition is a popular musical composition, and the sum of fifty (50¢) cents for each copyrighted musical composition embodied therein when such composition is a production or standard number or other than a popular musical composition. If for any reason whatsoever it is inconvenient to make a separate copy, then you are permitted to use those copies which you have already made, provided each such use made by each station on such nationally sponsored broadcast is counted as a separate copy and you collect and pay to me the sums herein provided as though separate

copies had been in fact made for each such use. The fees specified in this paragraph are fees for recording and reproduction of copies thereof and shall not be deemed to constitute in whole or in part fees for the right to perform said musical compositions or recordings or copies thereof.

6. Prior to your recording for the purpose of reproducing copies thereof of any copyrighted musical composition pursuant to the terms of this license, you will furnish me with a list thereof and I will promptly advise you of the category of each such composition and whether such musical compositions are available for recording and reproduction by you pursuant to this license. You shall make payment to me in accordance with the provisions of this license, prior to the last day of each month, of all sums due pursuant to this license for recordings released by you during the preceding month.

In the event any recordings or copies thereof made by you pursuant to this license are furnished by you to any space radio broadcast station and used by such broadcast station for nationally sponsored programs, you agree to require such station to furnish you not later than the 10th of each month, with a complete list of all uses on nationally sponsored programs made by such station during the preceding month of any of the recordings and copies thereof furnished by you, and you, in turn, will promptly thereafter furnish me with a complete report of such uses as are thus reported to you, and will transmit to me prior to the last day of the month, with the report as furnished, the full amount shown to be due by such report, in accordance with paragraph "5" hereof.

7. Each copy of a recording shall bear in some appropriate place and in some appropriate manner your name and address and a license legend to be approved by me in writing.

8. I further hereby agree for myself and for and on behalf of all of the publishers whom I represent as Agent and Trustee in connection with this agreement, that I shall not enter into any license agreement with any other person, firm or corporation for the use of copyrighted musical compositions on electrical transcriptions on terms more favorable to the licensee than those provided herein, and that in the event of any license agreement being entered into by me with any person, firm or corporation engaged in the business of manufacturing electrical transcriptions being deemed by you to be on terms more favorable to the licensee than those provided for herein, you may, upon your election, substitute such terms for the terms of this agreement, such substitution to be effective as of the date of such other agreement, and I agree to make such adjustments, financial and otherwise, as may be necessary to make the terms of the substituted agreement apply from such effective date.

Nothing herein contained shall deprive the publishers whom I represent as Agent and Trustee from acting independently.

9. The use of electrical transcriptions with respect to performances other than those which are public for profit, not having become generally established on a commercial basis, it is understood and agreed that nothing herein contained shall prejudice the rights of any of my principals or be construed as a precedent in the event the same hereafter shall become generally established, and any right to require additional or different recording fees in connection with such uses made under subsequent or superseding agreements, after the expiration of this agreement, hereby is reserved unto each of my principals individually.

10. This license is non-assignable and non-transferrable except that you may assign the same in whole or in part to any of your subsidiary or associated companies, provided that by so doing you are not relieved of any of your obligations hereunder.

11. This license is non-exclusive.

12. I agree on behalf of my principal or principals to hold you and your licensees and subscribers lawfully using such recordings and copies thereof manufactured pursuant hereto, such as a radio station or stations and others (including the sponsor and the advertising agency in the event that the transcriptions made by you hereunder are used in connection with locally or nationally sponsored broadcasts under paragraph "4" hereof), harmless and to indemnify you and them at all times against any and all judgments or recoveries arising from actions for infringements of copyrights or violations of common law property rights by reason of your recording or making copies thereof of any musical composition covered hereby, providing I or my

134

principal or principals are given the opportunity, at our own expense, to defend or join in the defense of any action or actions. In any event such obligation on behalf of my principals and the obligation of my principal or principals hereunder to indemnify and hold you and your licensees, subscribers and others harmless, shall not in any event exceed the amount of Two Hundred and Fifty ($250.00) Dollars with respect to any musical composition, which sum shall be payable jointly to you and to all such licensees, subscribers and others. Except as herein specifically provided, neither I nor the publisher or publishers assume any obligation or liability hereunder.

13. You hereby agree that if during the term of this agreement you enter into any agreement with any other person, firm or corporation, providing for the payment of a higher rate of royalty per musical composition than specified herein, that in such event my principals severally shall immediately have the right to receive thereafter, from the effective date of such other agreement, royalties at such higher rate in lieu of the royalties herein provided, and you agree to advise me of every such agreement within five (5) days after you have entered into the same. The provisions of this paragraph, however, shall not restrict your right to contract with any single publisher for the use of not more than five (5) musical compositions at a higher royalty rate, providing said agreement is made in good faith, and not for the purpose of circumventing the intention of this paragraph.

Dated: New York, N.Y.

CONSENTED AND AGREED TO:

Very truly yours,

_____   _____
                                                            HARRY FOX
                                                          Agent and Trustee

BY_____

Appendix T

ASCAP BACKGROUND MUSIC SERVICE LICENSE AGREEMENT

AGREEMENT made between the AMERICAN SOCIETY OF COMPOSERS, AUTHORS AND PUBLISHERS (hereinafter called "SOCIETY") and

a   Corporation (hereinafter called "LICENSEE"), as follows:

1. SOCIETY grants to LICENSEE and LICENSEE accepts, for the period commencing

and ending   , a non-exclusive license to publicly perform, or cause to be publicly performed, in the United States, its territories and possessions, non-visually, by means of "Background Music Service" (as hereinafter defined) and not otherwise, in the premises of "Subscribers of LICENSEE" (as hereinafter defined) and not elsewhere, non-dramatic renditions of the separate musical compositions of which SOCIETY shall, during the term hereof, have the right to license such performing rights. This license does not extend to or include the public performance of any rendition or performance of any opera, operetta, musical comedy, play or like production as such, in whole or in part.

Except as expressly herein otherwise provided, nothing herein contained shall be construed as authorizing LICENSEE to grant to others any right to reproduce or perform by any means, method or process whatsoever, any of the musical compositions licensed hereunder, or as authorizing "Subscribers of LICENSEE" (as hereinafter defined) to perform or reproduce compositions licensed hereunder by any method or process whatsoever except the reproduction and performance of such compositions by means of equipment at the premises of such "Subscribers of LICENSEE" (as hereinafter defined) designated in the agreement between each such respective Subscriber and LICENSEE.

The term "Background Music Service" as used in this agreement shall mean the transmission to the premises of "Subscribers of LICENSEE" (as hereinafter defined) of renditions of musical compositions, by means of

(a) wires or other conductors from a central studio or studios operated by LICENSEE and located at   ; or

(b) FM radio broadcasts from Station   , located at

or both, and the reproduction or performance of such renditions by means of equipment located in such premises.

Should LICENSEE's Background Music Service emanate from another FM radio station in lieu of or in addition to the one identified above, LICENSEE shall promptly identify such other FM radio station by written notice to SOCIETY and thereafter this agreement shall be deemed amended by the substitution or addition of the name of such other FM radio station for the station named hereinabove.

The term "Subscribers of LICENSEE", as used in this agreement, shall mean all persons, firms and corporations subscribing to the said Background Music Service.

This license shall not extend to or be deemed to include or authorize (a) the public performance of any musical composition licensed hereunder by any means, method or process whatsoever, other than those described above in this Paragraph "1"; or (b) the recording of, or the manufacture of, any recordings, or any other device used as a means of reproducing any musical composition of which the right of performance is licensed under this agreement.

2. This license shall not under any circumstances extend to (a) any ballroom, roller or ice-skating rink; or (b) any premises to which an admission fee is charged, provided, however, that this limitation shall apply only to the area of such premises from which the event or entertainment for which admission is charged is intended to be observed or heard and this license shall extend to any individual restaurant or store within any such premises where no separate admission fee is charged for admittance to such restaurant or store; or (c) transmission by any television station or any radio station to premises other than premises of Subscribers of LICENSEE; or (d) any community antenna operation.

3. A. LICENSEE warrants, represents and agrees that the fees set forth in Paragraph "6" of this agreement will be paid by LICENSEE with respect to all premises to which any Background Music Service is furnished directly or indirectly by LICENSEE or any enterprise which controls, is controlled by, or is under the same control as, LICENSEE.

B. LICENSEE further warrants and represents that each and every one of its agreements with its Subscribers hereafter made, as well as all renewals or extensions of existing agreements, will contain the following provision:

"The SUBSCRIBER shall not transmit the programs nor use the service outside the premises designated in this agreement."

4. LICENSEE warrants, represents and agrees and it is a condition of this license that no commercial announcements or advertising, of any kind, will be transmitted to or reproduced or disseminated in the premises of Subscribers of LICENSEE.

5. LICENSEE agrees to furnish to SOCIETY during the term of this agreement, commencing with the receipt of a written request therefor from the SOCIETY, a copy of the daily log, list or record of musical compositions transmitted during the term hereof by LICENSEE to such premises, showing the title of each composition and the composer and author thereof.

It is agreed that until ninety (90) days after such time as SOCIETY shall notify LICENSEE in writing to the contrary, it will be sufficient for LICENSEE to furnish to SOCIETY the printed form of program furnished by LICENSEE to its Subscribers.

6. In consideration of the license herein granted, LICENSEE agrees to pay to SOCIETY, with respect to each premises of each Subscriber of LICENSEE to which LICENSEE's Background Music Service is furnished, the following:

A. $27 per year for each premises of each Subscriber (other than the premises specifically mentioned in Sub-Paragraphs "B" and "C" of this Paragraph "6") including but not being limited to: hotels, motels, night clubs, restaurants, bars, grills, taverns, cocktail lounges and other establishments in which food and/or beverages are served, and stores, shops, supermarkets, automobile showrooms, gasoline service stations and other establishments where goods or services are sold or offered to the public at retail.

B. $27 per year for the first unit in each shopping center plus $15 per year for each additional unit in such shopping center.

Where LICENSEE's Background Music Service is furnished either to a Subscriber operating a shopping center where LICENSEE's Background Music Service is furnished to more than one unit, or to a Subscriber or Subscribers operating two or more such units within a shopping center, LICENSEE agrees that the amounts provided in this Sub-Paragraph "B" shall be paid with respect to each such unit in each such shopping center. For example if LICENSEE's Background Music Service were furnished to a total of 40 units in a total of 10 shopping centers, the fee would be:

$27.00 for the first unit in each of the 10 shopping centers	$27 × 10 =	$270
$15.00 for each of the remaining 30 units	$15 × 30 =	450
	Fee	$720

Each unit to which LICENSEE's Background Music Service is furnished by means of a speaker or speakers located immediately outside so as to render performances audible within such premises shall be treated the same as if the speaker or speakers were located inside such premises.

A "shopping center" as used in this agreement is a group of stores usually but not necessarily having common ownership, a related architectural style, and a common parking lot and not generally located in the central business area of a city. A group of stores shall not be deemed to be a shopping center merely by virtue of the fact that they are adjacent to one another. A "unit" in such a shopping center is a store, shop, supermarket, automobile showroom, gasoline service station or other establishment where goods or services are sold or offered to the public at retail.

C.   A sum equal to 3½% of the gross amount paid for the installation and use of equipment in, and the servicing of, and the furnishing of programs to the premises of Subscribers of LICENSEE for the following premises (excluding premises described in Sub-Paragraphs "A" and "B" of this Paragraph "6"): an office, factory or plant; a bank; an office or a professional building; a doctor's, dentist's or other professional office; a hospital, clinic, nursing or rest home or rehabilitation center; a funeral home or mortuary; a library, school, college or university; a church; a private club owned and operated by the members as a non-commercial venture; an apartment house or residence; a governmental office; a park or recreation area owned and operated by the government excluding private or commercial concessions or leased areas; a garage; a security or commodity broker; an insurance or real estate agency; a finance or loan office; a savings and loan association; a warehouse; a trucking terminal which is limited to operators of such trucks and maintenance men and to which other members of the public are not generally admitted; a research organization or laboratory; a room occupied solely as a rest room (or lounge); a room occupied solely as a reception or information area or an employees' cafeteria in such respective premises.

Where merchandise, services or any thing or service of value is received in lieu of or in addition to cash consideration for the installation and use of equipment in, and the servicing of, and furnishing of programs to any premises described in this Sub-Paragraph "C", the same shall be described and the reasonable value thereof determined and accounting made to SOCIETY on the same basis as if a regular billing had been made by LICENSEE therefor in a sum equal to such value, provided however, that the fee for each such premises shall in no event be less than Fifteen Dollars ($15) per year.

The term "gross amount paid for the installation and use of equipment in, and the servicing of, and furnishing of programs to the premises of Subscribers of LICENSEE", as used in this Sub-Paragraph "C" of this Paragraph "6", shall be deemed to include all payments made (other than a bona fide payment for the actual sale price of equipment), whether in money or in any other form, directly or indirectly, for installation and use of LICENSEE's facilities, and for any and all services (including programs) furnished to the premises of such Subscribers of LICENSEE in connection therewith, and whether such payment shall have been made directly to LICENSEE or to any other person, firm or corporation.   No deductions shall be permitted except the following:

(1) the part of the cost of initial installation at such premises which represents the actual amount expended by LICENSEE for labor or materials other than the actual equipment installed by LICENSEE at such premises for which LICENSEE bills the Subscriber at the approximate cost of such labor or materials or a lesser amount;

(2) the amount of tax collected (whether or not separately billed) by LICENSEE from Subscribers with respect to premises described in this Sub-Paragraph "C" solely for payment under Section 4251 of the 1954 Internal Revenue Code and any similar tax that may be imposed by Federal, State or Municipal Governments if such tax is imposed upon Subscribers and is actually collected from Subscribers and paid by LICENSEE to the Federal or a State or Municipal Government;

(3) the fees under this Sub-Paragraph "C".

D.   For each premises for which a fee is payable under Sub-Paragraph "A" or "B" of this Paragraph "6", and for which the agreement between the Subscriber of LICENSEE and LICENSEE shall commence on any day from the first through the fifteenth day of any month, or terminate on any day from the sixteenth through the last day of any month, the fee shall be paid in full for such month.   For each such premises for which such agreement shall commence on any day from the sixteenth through the last day of any month, or terminate on any day from the first through the fifteenth day of any month, no fee shall be payable for such month.

E.   The minimum fee under this agreement shall be Ten Dollars ($10) per month; provided, however, that if LICENSEE has not been engaged in the background music business for six (6) months, this provision shall not apply until LICENSEE shall have completed six (6) months in said business.

7.   LICENSEE agrees to render monthly statements to SOCIETY on or before the last day of each month, covering the period of the preceding calendar month, setting forth separately the gross amounts paid for the installation and use of equipment in, and the servicing of, and furnishing of programs to the premises of Subscribers of LICENSEE, without exception, for (a) all premises of all Subscribers and (b) all premises described in Paragraph "6.C."; the number of premises within Sub-Paragraph "6.A."; the number of shopping centers within Sub-Paragraph "6.B.", indicating as to each the number of units to which LICENSEE's Background Music Service is furnished; and the amount payable under Paragraph "6" of this agreement.   Whenever any deduction is made for the amount expended for labor or materials as provided in Paragraph "6.C.", an itemized statement of the amounts so expended shall be set forth.   Said statements shall be rendered under oath on forms supplied gratis by SOCIETY, and shall be accompanied by a remittance in full of the amount due SOCIETY under the terms hereof.

Accountings and payments shall be made on a billing basis with the right of reduction or rebate for bad accounts.   All billings made subsequent to the termination of this license with respect to installations, servicing or the furnishing of programs during the term hereof, shall be accounted for by LICENSEE as and when such billings shall be made by LICENSEE; and it is agreed that all such billings shall be made by LICENSEE not later than thirty (30) days after the termination of this license.

8. Society shall have the right by its duly authorized representatives, at any time during customary business hours, to examine the books and records of account of Licensee to such extent as may be necessary to verify any and all statements rendered and accountings made hereunder.

Society shall give Licensee not less than thirty (30) days' written notice of its intention to make such an examination. If, within ten (10) days after receipt of such written notice, Licensee shall give Society written notice of its desire to have the examination conducted by an independent certified public accountant, then (a) the examination shall be made by any nationally known certified accounting firm or by any independent certified public accountant residing in the state or within 100 miles of Licensee's principal place of business, selected by Society and (b) the total cost of such accounting firm or such an independent certified public accountant, including fees and expenses, shall be borne as follows: Society shall bear the first Two Hundred and Fifty Dollars ($250) of such cost, and the balance shall be borne equally by Licensee and by Society.

Licensee shall give Society's auditor (including any independent certified public accountant Society may select) full access to all relevant records of Licensee, including the names and addresses of, and any other pertinent information concerning, the Subscribers of Licensee. Society agrees to instruct auditors in its employ not to make any list of the names and addresses of Subscribers of Licensee except insofar as necessary for the verification of Licensee's statements and accountings to Society, and to destroy any such list upon completion of the audit or, if a deficiency be found as to which such data may be relevant, upon the payment or other disposition of such audit deficiency. Society agrees to instruct any independent certified public accountant selected by Society not to furnish any list of the names and addresses of Subscribers of Licensee, or any copy thereof, to Society or to anyone else.

9. Society reserves the right, at any time and from time to time, in good faith, to restrict the performance of compositions from musical comedies, operas, operettas, and motion pictures, or any other composition being excessively performed, only for the purpose of preventing harmful effect upon such musical comedies, operas, operettas, motion pictures or compositions, in respect of other interests under the copyrights thereof; provided, however, that the maximum number of compositions which may be at any time thus restricted shall not exceed three hundred (300) and moreover that limited licenses will be granted upon application entirely free of additional charge as to restricted compositions, if and when the copyright owners thereof are unable to show reasonable hazards to their major interests likely to result from such performances; and provided further that Society shall not exercise such right to restrict any such composition for the purpose of permitting the fixing or regulating of fees for the recording or transcribing of such composition; and provided further that in no case shall any charges, "free plugs" or other consideration be required in respect of any permission granted to perform a restricted composition; and provided further that in no event shall any composition, after the initial radio or television broadcast thereof, be restricted for the purpose of confining further performances thereof to a particular program or licensee.

Society reserves the further right, at any time and from time to time, in good faith, to restrict the performance of any compositions, over and above the number specified in the previous paragraph, only as to which any suit has been brought or threatened on a claim that such composition infringes a composition not contained in Society's repertory or on a claim that Society does not have the right to license the performing rights in such composition.

10. Upon any breach or default by Licensee of any terms herein contained, Society may give Licensee thirty (30) days notice in writing to cure such breach or default, and in the event such breach or default has not been cured within the said thirty (30) days, Society may then forthwith terminate this license.

11. Society agrees to indemnify, save and hold Licensee and the respective premises of Subscribers of Licensee harmless, and defend Licensee and such premises from and against any claim, demand or suit that may be made or brought against it with respect to renditions given on Licensee's programs during the term hereof in accordance with this license, of the separate musical compositions copyrighted or composed by members of Society and in Society's repertory.

In the event of the service upon Licensee or any such premises of any notice, process, paper or pleading, under which a claim, demand or action is made or begun against Licensee or any such premises on account of any such matter as is hereinabove referred to, Licensee shall promptly give Society written notice thereof and simultaneously therewith deliver to Society any such notice, process, paper or pleading, or a copy thereof, and Society at its own expense shall have sole charge of the defense of any such action or proceeding. Licensee, however, shall have the right to engage counsel of its own, at its own expense, who may participate in the defense of any such action or proceeding and with whom counsel for Society shall cooperate. Licensee shall cooperate with Society in every way in the defense of any such action or proceeding, and in any appeals that may be taken from any judgments or orders entered therein, and shall execute all pleadings, bonds or other instruments, but at the sole expense of Society, that may be required in order properly to defend and resist any such action or proceeding, and prosecute any appeals taken therein.

In the event of the service upon LICENSEE of any notice, process, paper or pleading under which a claim, demand or action is made or begun against LICENSEE on account of the rendition of any musical composition contained in SOCIETY's repertory but not copyrighted or composed by members of SOCIETY, SOCIETY agrees at the request of LICENSEE to cooperate with and assist LICENSEE in the defense of any such action or proceeding, and in any appeals that LICENSEE may elect to take from any judgments or orders entered therein.

12. All notices required or permitted to be given by either of the parties to the other hereunder shall be duly and properly given if mailed to such other party by registered or certified United States mail, addressed to such other party at its main office for the transaction of business.

13. If LICENSEE shall cease to operate the Background Music Service referred to in this agreement and if LICENSEE shall have discharged all the obligations of LICENSEE to SOCIETY under this agreement, then LICENSEE shall have the right to assign this agreement for the balance of its term upon the express condition that such assignee shall accept such assignment and shall agree to assume and to carry out and perform all the terms and conditions of this agreement on the part of LICENSEE to be kept and performed for the balance of the term of this agreement. Upon such acceptance and assumption, LICENSEE shall be relieved of any future obligations hereunder. Except as hereinabove expressly provided, LICENSEE shall have no right to transfer or assign this agreement, the rights granted hereunder being personal to LICENSEE.

IN WITNESS WHEREOF this agreement has been duly executed by SOCIETY and LICENSEE, this

day of , 19

AMERICAN SOCIETY OF COMPOSERS,
AUTHORS AND PUBLISHERS

By ....

....
LICENSEE

American Society of Composers,
    Authors and Publishers
575 Madison Avenue
New York, New York 10022

Gentlemen:

This refers to the Background Music Service agreement entered into simultaneously herewith.

With respect to Paragraph "4" of said agreement, it is understood that in the event we decide in the future to furnish a music service with commercial announcements, you shall offer, upon application by us to you, the then current form of license agreement offered to others similarly situated who furnish such a music service. If that form of agreement is acceptable to us, you and we agree to execute it promptly effective from the date we begin furnishing a music service with commercial announcements to any Subscriber. If that form of agreement is not acceptable to us, we shall promptly advise you of that fact and it is understood that our application to you shall be treated as an application under the Consent Decree in *United States of America* v. *American Society of Composers, Authors and Publishers,* and if we are unable to agree on reasonable rates as provided in that Consent Decree, we may apply thereunder to have the Court determine a reasonable fee for such a music service.

If, notwithstanding the provisions of Paragraph "4" of said agreement, any Subscriber shall insert commercial announcements in conjunction with our Background Music Service, such insertion shall not be deemed to be a breach of said agreement provided that we shall pay to you for each such Subscriber the sum of three dollars ($3.00) per month per floor for each month during which any such insertion shall be made, in lieu of all other fees payable under said agreement.

Nothing contained herein, or in Paragraph "4" of said agreement, shall be construed to deprive the Subscribers of LICENSEE of the right to insert public address announcements concerning goods or services sold or offered to the public at the premises of such Subscribers, where no compensation (in money or any other form) is paid to anyone, directly or indirectly, for such announcements. The fees provided in said agreement, rather than those provided in the preceeding paragraph, shall apply to the premises of Subscribers who insert such public address announcements.

Your signature in the space provided below shall constitute this a valid and enforceable agreement modifying as herein provided the terms and conditions of the said Background Music Service agreement.

Very truly yours,

ACCEPTED AND AGREED TO:

AMERICAN SOCIETY OF COMPOSERS,
    AUTHORS AND PUBLISHERS

By _____

Appendix U

BMI BACKGROUND MUSIC SERVICE
LICENSE AGREEMENT

AGREEMENT, made at New York, N. Y. this................day of............................, 19........... between BROADCAST MUSIC, INC., a corporation organized under the laws of the State of New York (hereinafter called BMI) with principal offices at 589 Fifth Ave., New York, N. Y., and..

doing business under the trade name of...

Strike Out } A corporation organized under the laws of ....
inapplicable } A partnership composed of ....
lines (An individual residing at ....

(hereinafter called LICENSEE) with offices located at ....

City of .... State of ....

WITNESSETH:

WHEREAS, BMI is engaged in licensing music for public performance for profit, and,

WHEREAS, LICENSEE, is engaged in the business of operating a background music service (hereinafter called "music service") which supplies a musical program service to individual places of entertainment, resort, residence, business, industry and others (all of which are hereinafter called "locations") in the territory hereinafter set forth,

IT IS HEREBY AGREED AS FOLLOWS:

1. (a) "Background Music" as used herein shall mean and be limited to non-dramatico performances of recorded music designed to be used as an unobtrusive accompaniment to work, shopping, conversation, dining and relaxation.

(b) "Locations" as used herein shall mean hotels, restaurants, bars, grills, taverns, factories, offices, banking institutions, stores, professional offices, residences and others, and shall not under any circumstances extend to (i) any ballroom or skating rink; or (ii) any premises to which an admission fee is charged, provided, however, that this limitation shall apply only to the area of such premises from which the event or entertainment for which admission is charged is intended to be observed or heard and this license shall extend to any individual restaurant or store within any such premises where no separate admission fee is charged for admittance to such restaurant or store; or (iii) transmission by any television station or any radio station to premises other than locations of LICENSEE; or (iv) any community antenna operation.

(c) "Industrial Locations" as used herein shall mean and be limited to factories, plants, businesses, banks and the like where music service is primarily confined to the personnel employed by the location or in retail establishments where music service is primarily confined to personnel areas during the hours when the store is open to the public or furnished through the store premises during such times when the store is not open to the public.

(d) "Other Locations" as used herein shall mean all locations which are not industrial locations as defined herein.

(e) "Contract year" as used herein shall mean any contract year of the term hereof and of any extended term as provided in paragraph 8 of this agreement.

(f) "Territory" as used herein shall mean and be limited to ....
....

2. BMI hereby grants to LICENSEE a non-exclusive license to perform publicly for profit and to cause or permit the public performance for profit by background music at locations within the territory of all musical works, the right to grant public performances of which BMI shall, during the term hereof control. Such performances shall be solely through LICENSEE's transmitting equipment and reproducing equipment installed on the locations of LICENSEE and by means of

    (a) wires or other conductors from a central studio located at...;

    (b) radio transmissions over the main or subsidiary channels of FM broadcasting station (insert call letters) ....located at ....;
and audible only within such locations and immediately adjacent thereto, and by no other means whatsoever and shall not extend or apply to performances associated with any advertising or announcements for which any payments are made to LICENSEE or locations or to any other performances whatsoever.

3. LICENSEE agrees to pay to BMI for each contract year of the term of this agreement or of any extended term during which music service is furnished to locations of LICENSEE a fee computed on the following basis, provided, however, that with the commencement of the second contract year of the term hereof the total payment to BMI for all locations to which music service is furnished shall not be less than Fifty ($50.00) Dollars for each contract year.

    (a) Industrial Locations . . . a sum equal to one-half percent ($\frac{1}{2}$%) of the gross amount charged or billed to any person, firm or corporation in the territory during the term of this agreement, but in no event less than Five ($5.00) Dollars per contract year for each such location to which music service is supplied during the term hereof or any extended term.

    (b) Other Locations except shopping centers . . . a sum equal to one percent (1%) of the gross amount charged or billed to any person, firm or corporation in the territory set forth herein but, except for small professional offices, residences, hospitals and governmental offices, in no event less than Five ($5.00) Dollars per contract year for each location to which music service is furnished during the term hereof or any extended term.

    (c) Shopping Centers . . . where LICENSEE furnishes music service to more than one location in a shopping center which is constructed and operated as a coordinated group of stores, a sum equal to one percent (1%) of the gross amount charged or billed to each such location but in no event less than Five ($5.00) Dollars per year for the first location in such shopping center and Three ($3.00) Dollars per year for every additional location contained therein to which music service is furnished during the term hereof or any extended term.

4. Payments shall be made quarter-annually on or before January 30th, April 30th, July 30th and October 30th, of each contract year of the term hereof or any extended term covering the preceding three-month period, or any part thereof, ending on the last day of the previous month. Payments shall be accompanied by a statement signed by either an officer or by the auditor of LICENSEE (on forms to be furnished by BMI) and such statement shall set forth the number of locations, the category of all locations, and all sums billed or charged during the period covered by the statement.

    (a) Such quarterly payments for each location (other than those contained in a shopping center, professional offices, residences, hospitals and governmental offices) shall not be less than One Dollar and Twenty-Five Cents ($1.25).

    (b) Such quarterly payments for locations contained in a shopping center shall not be less than One Dollar and Twenty-Five Cents ($1.25) for the first location therein and Seventy-Five Cents ($.75) for each additional location therein.

    (c) At the end of each contract year of the term hereof or of any extended term, the applicable percentage of the gross billings, less credits, allowances and deductions, for each contract year as provided in each of the sub-paragraphs (a), (b) and (c) of paragraph 3 hereof shall be calculated and if the resultant amount is in excess of the aggregate amount of the minimum fees for all locations to which music service was furnished during such contract year as set forth in sub-paragraphs (a) and (b) of this paragraph 4, LICENSEE shall pay BMI the amount of such excess.

5. BMI agrees to credit LICENSEE with fees paid for any location for any period during which such location is already licensed by BMI to perform the music contained in its repertory by live musicians actually on the premises, provided, LICENSEE, at the time of furnishing BMI with quarter-annual statements, shall submit a list containing the names and addresses of locations which LICENSEE claims are performing live music by means of musicians actually present on the premises. Upon receipt of such list, BMI shall promptly advise LICENSEE which locations in such list are presently licensed by BMI for the public performance of live music on the premises, and BMI shall at the same time issue to LICENSEE a statement of the appropriate credits for such locations. LICENSEE may deduct the amount of such credits from its payment to BMI for the following quarter-annual period.

6. LICENSEE may make deductions for bad accounts, provided, LICENSEE, at the time of taking such deductions, shall furnish BMI with specific information as to each deduction, but in no event shall LICENSEE make such deductions until the accounts have been charged off on the books of LICENSEE as bad debts.

7. The gross amount paid for the installation and use of equipment in, and the servicing of, and furnishing of music service to said locations, shall be deemed to include all payments made (other than a bona fide payment for the actual sale price of equipment), whether in money or in any other form, directly or indirectly, for installation and use of LICENSEE's facilities, and for any and all services (including programs) furnished to the said locations and whether such payment shall have been made directly to LICENSEE or to any other person, firm or corporation. In making payments, LICENSEE may exclude only the following:

(a) the part of the cost of initial installation at such locations which represents the actual amount expended by LICENSEE for labor or materials other than the actual equipment installed by LICENSEE at such locations for which LICENSEE bills the location at the approximate cost of such labor or materials or a lesser amount;

(b) the amount of the tax payable under Section 4251 of the Internal Revenue Code and any similar tax that may be imposed by State or Municipal Governments if such tax is paid by the location and separately billed therefor;

(c) the fees paid to BMI pursuant to this agreement.

8. The term of this agreement shall commence as of.. and end on
.... This agreement shall be automatically extended and renewed for further periods of one year each, from year to year, after the expiration of the foregoing term or any extended term hereof unless either party, on or before ninety (90) days next preceding the termination of the foregoing term or any extended term, shall give notice to the other in writing by United States registered mail of the desire to terminate the same at the conclusion of such term.

9. BMI shall have the right by its duly authorized representatives, at any time during customary business hours, to examine the books and records of account of LICENSEE to such extent as may be necessary to verify any and all statements rendered and accountings made hereunder.

BMI shall give LICENSEE not less than thirty (30) days written notice of its intention to make such an examination. If, within ten (10) days after receipt of such written notice, LICENSEE shall give BMI written notice of its desire to have the examination conducted by an independent auditor, the examination shall be made by any nationally known accounting firm or by any independent auditor residing in the State or within 100 miles of LICENSEE's principal place of business, selected by BMI.

LICENSEE shall give BMI's auditor (including any independent auditor BMI may select) full access to all relevant records of LICENSEE, including the names and addresses of, and any other pertinent information concerning, the locations of LICENSEE. BMI agrees to instruct auditors in its employ not to make any list of the names and addresses of the locations of LICENSEE except insofar as necessary for the verification of LICENSEE's statements and accountings to BMI, and to destroy any such list upon completion of the audit or, if a deficiency be found as to which such data may be relevant, upon the payment or other disposition of such audit deficiency. BMI agrees to instruct any independent auditor selected by BMI not to furnish any list of the names and addresses of locations of LICENSEE, or any copy thereof, to BMI or to anyone else.

10. BMI agrees to indemnify, save harmless and defend LICENSEE and the proprietors of the locations serviced by it hereunder, from and against any and all claims, demands or suits that may be made or brought against them, or any of them, with respect to the performance under this license agreement of any material licensed hereunder. Such indemnity shall specifically apply to all works which appear in the current catalog and lists of BMI as corrected and modified. Such indemnity shall not apply to works performed at the locations serviced by LICENSEE after written request by BMI that LICENSEE's locations refrain from such performances. LICENSEE agrees to give BMI immediate notice of any such claim or suit, either against it or against any location serviced by it, to deliver to BMI any papers pertaining thereto, and to cooperate and to cause the locations serviced by it to cooperate with respect thereto, and BMI shall have full charge of the defense of any such claim, demand or suit. LICENSEE shall have the right to engage counsel of its own, at its own expense, who may participate in the defense of any such action or proceeding and with whom counsel for BMI shall cooperate. LICENSEE shall cooperate with BMI in every way in the defense of any such action or proceeding, and in any appeals that may be taken from any judgments or orders entered therein, and shall execute all pleadings, bonds or other instruments, but at the sole expense of BMI, that may be required in order properly to defend and resist any such action or proceeding, and prosecute any appeals taken therein.

11. LICENSEE agrees to furnish to BMI monthly, throughout the term hereof, in the event that BMI shall so request in writing, a copy of the log, list or record of musical compositions transmitted or furnished to its locations during the term hereof within the territory hereinabove defined.

12. In the event that BMI, during the term of this agreement, shall issue licenses on a formula or other basis more favorable to similar background music licensees than are contained herein, such more favorable license agreements shall be tendered to LICENSEE.

13. It is agreed that LICENSEE may assign this agreement to any subsidiary, affiliated or associated company of LICENSEE or in connection with any sale, merger, reorganization or consolidation in which LICENSEE is a party.

14. Any notice required or permitted to be given under this agreement shall be in writing and shall be deemed duly given when sent by ordinary U.S. mail to the party for whom it is intended, at its address hereinabove stated, or any other address which either party hereto may from time to time designate for such purpose, and when any such notice is so mailed, it shall be deemed to have been given upon the mailing thereof.

15. Upon any breach or default by the LICENSEE of any term or condition herein contained, BMI may, at its sole option, and in addition to any and all other remedies which it may have at law or in equity, cancel this license upon ten days notice in writing to LICENSEE, addressed to the licensed premises. No waiver by BMI of full performance of this license by LICENSEE in any one or more instances shall be deemed a waiver of the right to require full and complete performance of this license thereafter or of the right to cancel this license in accordance with the terms of this paragraph.

16. This agreement constitutes the entire understanding between the parties with respect to the subject matter hereof. This agreement cannot be waived or added to or modified orally and no waiver, addition or modification shall be valid unless in writing and signed by the parties. This agreement, its validity, construction and effect shall be governed by the laws of the State of New York.

IN WITNESS WHEREOF, the parties hereto have duly executed this agreement the day and year hereinabove set forth.

BROADCAST MUSIC, INC.

By ....

....
LICENSEE

By ....

....
TITLE

Appendix V

FORM OF TELEVISION FILM SYNCHRONIZATION LICENSE

TV License No.:   Date:

Composition:

To Licensee:

1. In consideration of the sum of_____payable upon the execution hereof, we grant you the non-exclusive right to record on film or video tape the above identified musical composition(s) in synchronization or timed relation with a single episode or individual program entitled_____ for television use only, subject to all of the terms and conditions herein provided.

2. (a) The type of use is to be_____
    (b) On or before the first telecast of the said film, you or your assigns agree to furnish to us a copy of the cue sheet prepared and distributed in connection therewith.

3. The territory covered by this license is the world.

4. (a) This license is for a period of_____from the date hereof.
    (b) Upon the expiration of this license all rights herein granted shall cease and terminate and the right to make or authorize any further use or distribution of any recordings made hereunder shall also cease and terminate.

5. This is a license to record only and does not authorize any use of the aforesaid musical composition(s) not expressly set forth herein. By way of illustration but not limitation, this license does not include the right to change or adapt the words or to alter the fundamental character of the music of said musical composition(s) or to use the title(s) thereof as the title or sub-title of said film.

6. Performance of the said musical composition(s) in the exhibition of said film is subject to the condition that each television station over which the aforesaid musical composition(s) is (are) to be so performed shall have a performance license issued by us or from a person, firm, corporation, society, association or other entity having the legal right to issue such performance license.

7. No sound records produced pursuant to this license are to be manufactured, sold and/or used separately or independently of said film.

8. The film shall be for television use only but may not be televised into theatres or other places where admission is charged.

9. All rights not herein specifically granted are reserved by us.

10. We warrant only that we have the legal right to grant this license and this license is given and accepted without other warranty or recourse. If said warranty shall be breached in whole or in part with respect to (any of) said musical composition(s), our total liability shall be limited either to repaying to you the consideration theretofore paid under this license with respect to such musical composition to the extent of such breach or to holding you harmless to the extent of the consideration theretofore paid under this license with respect to such musical composition to the extent of said breach.

146

11. This license shall run to you, your successors and assigns, provided you shall remain liable for the performance of all of the terms and conditions of this license on your part to be performed and provided further that any disposition of said film or any prints thereof shall be subject to all the terms hereof, and you agree that all persons, firms or corporations acquiring from you any right, title, interest in or possession of said film or any prints thereof shall be notified of the terms and conditions of this license and shall agree to be bound thereby.

MUSIC PUBLISHER

By_____

Appendix W

FORM OF SOUND TRACK LIBRARY
SYNCHRONIZATION LICENSE

Library, Inc. hereby grants to the undersigned Licensee as the authorized representative of the producer, or as the producer, of the production entitled_____ (the music cue sheet of which Licensee agrees to furnish to Library, Inc.) the non-exclusive irrevocable right, license, privilege and authority to use the recordings listed below for the sole, limited and restricted purpose of including said recordings and mechanically reproducing the same in connection with the said production as an integral part thereof and the exhibition or broadcast of said production as a (television) (theatrical) (industrial) film in the following territory only:

		PUBLISHER
NUMBER TITLE	COMPOSER	(PERFORMANCE RIGHTS)
_____	_____	_____
_____	_____	_____
_____	_____	_____
_____	_____	_____

This is a license to record only and the public performance for profit of the said production is subject to the rights, if any, of the various composers or performing rights societies or other owners of the performing rights in the music to collect performing fees therefor. Library, Inc. represents and warrants only that it is the sole owner or authorized agent of the owner of the recordings covered by this license and agrees to repay the consideration paid for this license if said warranty shall be breached. Licensee agrees that this license is granted without any other warranty or recourse.

(LICENSEE)   LIBRARY, INC.

BY_____   BY_____

Appendix X

MINIMUM COMPENSATION AND PUBLICATION ROYALTY PROVISIONS IN PRODUCERS-COMPOSERS AND LYRICISTS GUILD OF AMERICA MINIMUM BASIC AGREEMENT OF 1965

ARTICLE 20 MINIMUM COMPENSATION

(a) Definition of a qualified composer and song writer:

(1) A qualified composer of underscoring is a composer who has screen credit for one feature length picture, three one-half (½) hour or one one-hour (1) or more in length television motion picture, or 52 weeks of employment in the motion picture industry, as a composer of underscoring.

(2) A qualified song composer is a composer who has two published songs or who composed two separate songs each of which is completely contained in a motion picture produced and released in the American motion picture industry or who has had 52 weeks of employment in the American motion picture industry as a composer of either or both song music or song lyrics.

(b) Wage Scale Minimum Compensation:

(1) There are no minimum compensation requirements with respect to unqualified composers.

(2) The minimum compensation per week for a qualified composer for composition only, shall be:

	Television Motion Pictures	Theatrical Motion Pictures
Term contract:	$325.00	$357.50
Week to week:	$350.00	$385.00

The above salary shall commence and apply when an assignment is made under the Producer's direction and control. The above television weekly rate shall apply in term or week-to-week employment in any week in which no work hereunder is performed in a theatrical motion picture; in any week in which such work is performed in both theatrical and television motion pictures the theatrical motion picture rate will apply for that week. For these purposes, a term contract is a personal service contract for a term of at least ten out of thirteen weeks or any like ratio for a longer period. A week-to-week contract is a personal service contract for a term of less than ten out of thirteen weeks. A composer employed on a weekly basis, may be terminated at any time after one week.

If any composer under a week-to-week or term contract shall render services after the expiration of the period for which his specified compensation is provided in the employment contract and no additional amount is specified for such additional period, then in such event the composer shall receive the weekly rate specified in such contract for each week, or, for purpose only of prorating days worked in a partial workweek (of less than six (6) days), one-fifth (1/5) for each such a day worked during which the composer shall render such additional services. In any week of employment when the Producer may under this agreement employ the composer for less than one full week (i.e. after one week or after the term of the agreement), if the composer shall render services in composition and also other services not covered by this agreement his minimum compensation for composition shall be prorated in proportion to the amount of time required by Producer for composition.

(3) In the alternative, when the employment for composition, excluding songs, is for television films only, and it is non-exclusive employment, the minimum compensation shall be:

a) Not less than $175 for a half-hour show.
b) Not less than $350 for a one-hour show.
c) Not less than $500 for a one and one-half hour show.
d) Not less than $20 per minute for a five-minute or less fragment, with minimum guarantee of not less than three minutes ($60).

The above rates of $175 for a half-hour show and $350 for an hour show shall be applicable where more than five minutes of new music is composed for a program.

Where more than five minutes of new music is composed and more than one composer is employed, the combined payments to such composers shall be not less than $175 for a half-hour show or $350 for an hour show. In no event shall a composer who composes five minutes or less of new music, under such circumstances, be paid less than the per minute rate applicable if he composed "a five minute or less fragment."

(4) The minimum compensation for employment for the composition of songs shall be governed by the theatrical rate provisions of (b) (2) of this article only.

(5) Any amounts paid to the composer in excess of the minimum compensation, as provided above, may be applied to any other payments required under this agreement.

(6) Theatrical Exhibition of Television Films:

In the event a television motion picture or pictures containing music composed on or after the effective date of this agreement, under the provisions of Article 20 (b) (3) above, is exhibited theatrically (as one or in combination) Producer shall pay to the composer or composers of such music, so used, in such exhibition, the following applicable single amount for an unlimited number of such exhibitions:

The amount, if any, that (i) $350 exceeds the compensation paid such composer or composers for a half hour show so used; or (ii) $700 exceeds the compensation paid such composer or composers employed for a one hour show so used, or (iii) $1,000 exceeds the compensation paid such composer or composers employed for a one and one-half hour show so used; or (iv) $40 exceeds the compensation paid such composer or composers employed for each minute for a five-minute or less fragment so used.

ARTICLE 21 PUBLICATION ROYALTIES

Should the Producer, or any subsidiary or affiliated company, or any assignee or licensee of Producer, exploit the music or musical composition (hereinafter referred to as the "composition") then the Producer, or such subsidiary or affiliated company, or such assignee or licensee, shall pay directly to the composer an amount of royalty with respect to such composition not less than the following, and Producer's contract with such subsidiary or affiliated company, or assignee or licensee, shall so require and if Producer's contract does so provide then Producer shall not be responsible for payment of the royalties hereunder:

(a) Five cents (5¢) per copy in respect of regular piano copies sold and paid for in the United States and Canada.

(b) Fifty percent (50%) of all net sums received by the publisher in respect of regular piano copies, orchestrations, band arrangements, octavos, quartets, arrangements for combinations of voices and/or instruments, and/or other copies of the composition sold in any country other than the United States and Canada; provided, however, that if the publisher should sell such copies through, or cause them to be sold by, a subsidiary or affiliate or any assignee or licensee which is actually doing business in a foreign country, then in respect of such sales, the publisher shall pay to the composer not less than ten percent (10%) of the wholesale selling price in respect of each such copy sold and paid for.

150

(c) Ten percent (10%) of the wholesale selling price (after trade discounts if any) of each copy sold and paid for in the United States and Canada, or for export from the United States, of orchestrations, band arrangements, octavos, quartets, arrangements for combinations of voices and/or instruments, and/or other copies of the composition (other than regular piano copies).

(d) (i) If the composition, or any part thereof, is included in any song book, song sheet, folio or similar publication issued by the publisher containing at least four (4), but not more than twenty-five (25) musical compositions, the royalty to be paid by the publisher to the composer shall be an amount determined by dividing ten percent (10%) of the wholesale selling price (after trade discounts, if any) of the copies sold, among the total number of copyrighted musical compositions included in such publication. If such publication contains more than twenty-five (25) musical compositions, said ten percent (10%) shall be increased by an additional one-half percent (½) for each additional musical composition.

(ii) If, pursuant to a license granted by the publisher to a licensee not controlled by or affiliated with it, the composition, or any part thereof, is included in any song book, song sheet, folio or similar publication, containing at least four (4) musical compositions, the royalty to be paid by the publisher to the composer shall be that proportion of fifty percent (50%) of the gross amount received by it from the licensee, as the number of uses of the composition under the license and during the license period, bears to the total number of uses of the publisher's copyrighted musical compositions under the license and during the license period. Such royalties shall be computed and paid within thirty (30) days after the expiration of the term of each license, but if any such license term is in excess of one year, such royalties shall be computed and paid annually.

(iii) In computing the number of the publisher's copyrighted musical compositions under subdivision (ii) hereof, there shall be excluded musical compositions in the public domain and arrangements of musical compositions in the public domain if no royalties are payable with respect to such arrangements by the publisher.

(iv) Royalties on publications containing less than four (4) musical compositions shall be payable at regular piano copy rates.

(e) As to "professional material" not sold or resold, no royalty shall be payable.

(f) Fifty percent (50%) of all net sums actually received by the publisher in respect of any licenses (including statutory royalties) authorizing the manufacture of parts of instruments serving to mechanically reproduce the composition; or to use the composition in synchronization with sound motion pictures produced by anyone other than: (i) the Producer, its subsidiary, and affiliated companies; (ii) any company using the composition in a motion picture financed substantially by or to be distributed by the Producer; and (iii) the producer for whom the composition was originally composed, and its subsidiary and affiliated companies; or to reproduce it upon electrical transcription for broadcasting purposes; except that the composer(s) shall not be entitled to any share of the monies distributed to the publisher by any performing rights society anywhere in the world, or other source, which makes a distribution to composers either directly or through another performing rights society or other person, company, society, association or organization.

(g) If the publisher administers licenses authorizing the manufacture of parts of instruments serving to mechanically reproduce said composition, or the use of said composition in synchronization or in timed relation with sound motion pictures produced by anyone other than: (i) the Producer, its subsidiary, and affiliated companies; (ii) any company using the composition in a motion picture financed substantially by or to be distributed by the Producer; and (iii) the producer for whom the composition was originally composed, and its subsidiary and affiliated companies; or its reproduction upon electrical transcriptions, or any of them, through an agent, trustee or other administrator acting for a substantial part of the industry and not under the exclusive control of the publisher (hereinafter sometimes referred to as licensing agent), the publisher in determining his receipts, shall be entitled to deduct from gross license fees paid by the licensees, a sum equal to the charges paid by the publisher to said licensing agent.

The foregoing rates shall apply only in cases in which all of the music and lyrics of the composition have been composed by one composer, or in cases in which a musical composition has been composed for which no lyrics have been written.

As to songs, if one person composes the music and another the lyrics, the foregoing rates shall apply, but one-half shall be allocated to the composer of the music and one-half to the author of the lyrics (no allowances being made for the title). If there shall be more than one composer or more than one lyricist, then they shall agree between themselves upon the division of their half of the above royalties, but in the absence of such agreement, their half shall be divided equally between them.

The royalties hereinabove provided for shall be payable only in connection with compositions originally created by the composer, it being agreed that no royalties shall be payable with reference to arrangements, orchestrations, translations or other adaptations or modifications of compositions written by others.

No royalties shall be payable for any uses made by the Producer or by the independent producer for whom the composition was originally composed (or by its or their associated, affiliated, parent or subsidiary corporations or by any persons, firms or other corporations with whom or with which any of said corporations may have contracts or arrangements for the production, performance, television, exhibition or distribution of motion pictures) in motion pictures (theatrical or television) or in connection with any advertising, publicizing or exploitation thereof. Nothing in this agreement shall be construed to obligate the Producer or its licensees or assigns to publish, record, reproduce or otherwise exploit any music or musical composition.

Appendix Y

SAMPLE SOUND TRACK LIBRARY RATE CARD

XYZ PRODUCTION MUSIC
Schedule of Rates for Music Licensing

TELEVISION PRODUCTIONS,
INDUSTRIAL, RELIGIOUS, EDUCATIONAL AND OTHER
NON-THEATRICAL FILMS

A. Basic rate is $20 per track (i.e. per needle down) of music used or portion thereof and a maximum payment for any one film as follows:

Maximum Per Film	*Playing Time*
$ 60.00	Under 10 minutes
90.00	10 minutes thru 15 minutes
120.00	16 minutes thru 20 minutes
175.00	21 minutes thru 30 minutes
275.00	31 minutes thru 45 minutes
350.00	46 minutes thru 60 minutes

and with a reduced rate of $125 per film for thirteen or more half-hour films produced within a six month period.

NOTE: The rates given above cover television or non-theatrical licensing, but not both. To obtain both television *and* non-theatrical clearance, an additional sum equal to one-third of the original payment shall be due.

B. Theatrical and Subscription-System Productions: Rates available upon request.

C. Transcribed Radio Programs: $15 for each 15 minutes of program running time, or portion thereof.

D. Television and Transcribed Radio Spot Announcements: Regional/National, 3 minutes or less, $25 per track or portion thereof used. $150 maximum. Local, 3 minutes or less, $12.50 per track, $75 maximum.

E. Sound Discs for Slide Films: $12.50 per track, or portion thereof used.

F. Narrative Discs: $15 per track, or portion thereof used.

Appendix Z

FORM OF TAPE CARTRIDGE DUPLICATION AND DISTRIBUTION AGREEMENT

THIS AGREEMENT is made this_____day of_____by and between TAPE CARTRIDGE COMPANY (hereinafter called "Tape Company"), and RECORD COMPANY (hereinafter called "Licensor").

WHEREAS, Tape Company desires to sponsor and promote a central source for duplicating and distributing purposes of tape cartridges containing stereophonic magnetic sound tape recordings embodying performances of music played by a continuous loop process; and

WHEREAS, to implement this program, Tape Company desires to duplicate, package and distribute such tape cartridges made from recorded masters and duplicates; and

WHEREAS, Licensor desires to give to Tape Company the right to duplicate and distribute its music in tape cartridge form;

NOW, THEREFORE, in consideration of the premises and of the mutual agreements of the parties hereto, it is agreed as follows:

1. Licensor hereby grants Tape Company the exclusive right and license to reproduce, manufacture, distribute and sell continuous loop tape cartridges in the United States of America only, containing performances embodied in Licensor's master recordings which have been and may be hereafter released by Licensor and which are not restricted by contractual obligations. No reel-to-reel tape rights or record club tape rights are granted.

2. Licensor further grants Tape Company the right and license to reproduce Licensor's artwork and use Licensor's trademark upon tape cartridges manufactured and sold hereunder and upon the containers in which they are offered for sale, and in advertising and display material used for the sale thereof; and Tape Company agrees to use only such artwork and trademark except that Tape Company may use on the cartridge and container the legend, "Duplicated by Tape Company" or words of similar import, provided that such legend is not featured. Any deviation from the foregoing shall be approved in writing by Licensor. Tape Company agrees to submit for Licensor's review under the foregoing standards a sample of the proposed use of Tape Company's legend, prior to actual use thereof.

3. The term hereof shall be the period of one year commencing on the date of this agreement.

4. Licensor shall deliver to Tape Company, free of charge, three (3) sample pressings of all master recordings released by Licensor as album phonograph records. Tape Company shall notify Licensor of the particular recordings which Tape Company desires to release in tape cartridge form.

Promptly following such notice, Licensor shall deliver to Tape Company the appropriate original master tapes or copies thereof. Tape Company shall reimburse Licensor for actual costs involved, including the expenses of packing, shipping and insurance.

5. All tapes or duplicates thereof of recordings hereunder and all copyrights, ownerships and rights in and to such recordings shall remain the sole and exclusive property of Licensor, subject, however, to the rights of Tape Company to make reproductions pursuant to the terms of this agreement.

154

6. (a) In consideration for the rights herein granted, Tape Company agrees to pay Licensor royalties of_____per cent of ninety (90%) per cent of the suggested retail list price (exclusive of all excise and sales taxes) of all tape cartridges duplicated and sold by Tape Company. There shall be no deduction for tape cartridges returned by purchasers. Promotion copies for reviewers shall not be subject to royalty payments.

(b) In no event shall the royalty payable per LP utilized in a tape cartridge be less than _____cents for each tape cartridge duplicated and sold by Tape Company.

(c) In the computation of royalties there shall be deducted from the suggested retail list price_____cents for the costs of the container.

7. The royalties to be paid by Tape Company to Licensor hereunder are intended to include provision for all recording artists' and other talent royalties which shall be entirely payable by Licensor. Tape Company shall be free of any obligations to pay the costs of recording sessions.

8. Tape Company agrees to pay all mechanical license fees due to copyright proprietors of the music contained in tape cartridges produced hereunder.

9. With respect to cartridges manufactured or sold hereunder from master recordings which were produced subject to the American Federation of Musicians Music Performance Trust Fund Agreement, Tape Company agrees to pay or cause to be paid directly to such Fund all sums which may be or become due in accordance with such agreement, and agrees to pay or cause to be paid directly to the Special Fund established under the American Federation of Musicians Phonograph Record Labor Agreement (1964-1969) all sums which become due to such Fund.

10. Tape Company, in the performance of its obligations hereunder, undertakes to produce a finished tape cartridge of a quality that will meet Licensor's recording standards and satisfy Licensor that duplication of tapes for tape cartridges is done to its satisfaction. Licensor may select the person or firm to whom samples of such tape cartridges may be submitted for quality control purposes. Tape Company will supply Licensor with two (2) copies of each tape cartridge released, promptly after release.

11. Tape Company agrees to release tape cartridges of a minimum of_____ Licensor's albums during the term of this contract.

12. Tape Company shall have the right to use in the Licensed Territory the name, likeness and biography of each artist whose performance is embodied in the master recordings in connection with the advertising, publicizing or sale of cartridge tapes manufactured therefrom, provided, however, that Tape Company shall abide by any restrictions imposed upon Licensor with respect of which Licensor has notified Tape Company in writing at the time of delivery under paragraph 4.

13. All recordings released hereunder shall be released in their entirety and without editing and in the manner and for the purpose originally recorded by or for Licensor, unless Licensor's prior written consent is secured. There shall be no coupling of recordings without Licensor's consent.

14. Tape Company agrees to sell Licensor, pursuant to Licensor's order from time to time, tape cartridges manufactured by Tape Company hereunder at a discount of_____per cent from the suggested retail list price.

15. Licensor warrants that it is the sole and exclusive owner of the master recordings or is authorized to grant the rights herein granted by Licensor and that except as stated in writing to Tape Company it has full and complete rights in respect of any and all artists whose performances appear on said master recordings and that it is under no disability, restriction or prohibition in respect of its right to execute this agreement and perform its obligations hereunder or to grant the rights herein granted by Licensor.

16. It is understood that Tape Company is making comparable agreements with other firms and companies for the duplication, packaging and distribution of music in tape cartridges and that such companies may be competitive with Licensor. However, Tape Company agrees to treat

Licensor's recordings as one of its top lines and to devote to it promotional and sales efforts and advertising expenditures consistent with such treatment.

17. With respect to royalties provided for by paragraph 6 hereof, Tape Company shall render to Licensor complete and detailed accounting statements within forty-five (45) days after December 31, March 31, June 30 and September 30, respectively, of each year during which tape cartridges are made or sold hereunder. Such statements shall be accompanied by a remittance of the amount shown therein due to Licensor. Licensor may inspect and make extracts of the books and records of Tape Company and its subsidiaries and affiliates regarding any of the matters hereunder.

18. Either party shall have the right to terminate this agreement in the event that the other party hereto goes into liquidation, whether voluntary or involuntary, or takes the benefit of any insolvency law, or is judicially declared insolvent or bankrupt, or if a receiver shall be appointed for all or a substantial part of such party's assets or business.

19. If Tape Company fails to account and make payments hereunder and such failure is not cured within thirty (30) days after written notice thereof to Tape Company, or if Tape Company fails to perform any other obligations required of it hereunder and such failure is not cured within thirty (30) days after written notice thereof to Tape Company, then and in any of such events Licensor, in addition to such other rights or remedies which it may have at law or otherwise under this agreement, may elect to cancel or terminate this agreement without prejudice to any rights or claims it may have, and all rights hereunder shall forthwith revert to Licensor and Tape Company may not thereafter manufacture tape cartridges from master recordings furnished by Licensor or sell such tape cartridges. Tape Company shall degauss all such manufactured tape cartridges in its possession and thereupon return all then existing master tapes previously received from Licensor or any derivatives of same.

20. Written notification of termination to be issued to the parties hereunder shall be addressed as follows:

If to Tape Company:

If to Licensor:

21. Upon the termination hereof whether by reason of expiration of said term or pursuant to any other provision respecting termination, all manufacturing by Tape Company shall cease. With respect to all master tapes, including any made by Tape Company and any other material in Tape Company's hands used in the manufacture of Licensor's tape cartridges, Tape Company shall promptly at the option of Licensor and upon its written instructions either —

    (a) deliver same to Licensor, as designated by Licensor, at Licensor's sole cost and expense of delivery, or

    (b) destroy same under Licensor's supervision, or at Licensor's request destroy same and supply Licensor with an affidavit of such fact, sworn to by a principal officer of Licensor.

Subject to the provisions of paragraph 19, Tape Company shall have the right for a period of six months from and after the date of termination to dispose, in the regular course of business, of its inventory of finished tape cartridges on hand as of the date of termination, providing that Tape Company pays to Licensor the royalties required to be made and paid by Tape Company hereunder, and providing and on condition that within fifteen (15) days from such termination Tape Company furnishes to Licensor a written list of such inventory which also shows the factory cost thereof.

However, at any time after such termination, Licensor shall have the right to purchase from Tape Company at its factory cost all or part of the inventory not theretofore sold by Tape Company. Such sales shall not be subject to the payment of royalties under this agreement.

22. Tape Company agrees to defend, indemnify and hold Licensor harmless against any and all liability, loss, damage, cost or expense, including reasonable attorney's fees, paid or incurred

156

by reason of any breach or claim of breach of any of Tape Company's covenants, warranties or representations hereunder, or by reason of and in respect of the distribution, manufacture, sale or performance of tape cartridges made by Tape Company hereunder and not due to any violation or breach by Licensor of its covenants, warranties or representations hereunder.

23. In the interpretation and construction of this agreement, the laws of the State of New York applicable to agreements to be wholly performed therein shall apply.

24. Tape Company may not sublicense any of the rights granted to it hereunder.

25. This contract constitutes the entire agreement between Tape Company and Licensor and cannot be changed orally.

26. Notwithstanding the provisions of paragraph 1 hereof, Tape Company is authorized to sell finished tape cartridge product manufactured hereunder to Licensor's franchised foreign licensees, who are franchised at the time of sale, subject to the right of Licensor to cancel such authorization at any time upon thirty (30) days written notice. If such foreign licensees do not wish to distribute Tape Company's tape cartridge product, and the said licensees consent thereto, Licensor will negotiate with Tape Company for it to sell such product directly in the particular country, provided that Tape Company has an established and suitable marketing arrangement there.

IN WITNESS WHEREOF, the parties hereto have entered into this agreement the day and year first above written.

TAPE CARTRIDGE COMPANY

BY_____

RECORD COMPANY

BY_____

INDEX